HOLY Angels

SILVANUS OLUOCH

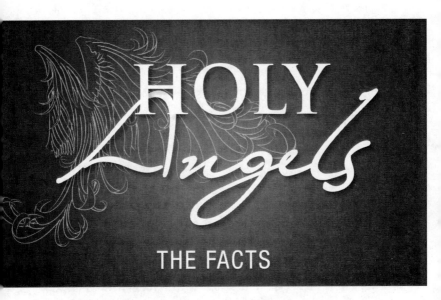

HOLY Angels

THE FACTS

Clear And Specific Information On God's Invisible Agents

Tate Publishing & Enterprises

Published by Tate Publishing & Enterprises, LLC
127 E. Trade Center Terrace | Mustang, Oklahoma 73064 USA
1.888.361.9473 | www.tatepublishing.com

Tate Publishing is committed to excellence in the publishing industry. The company reflects the philosophy established by the founders, based on Psalm 68:11,
"The Lord gave the word and great was the company of those who published it."

Published in the United States of America

ISBN: 978-1-60696-632-7
1. Religion / Christian Theology / Angelology & Demonology
09.01.28

The Son of man shall come in his glory, and all the holy angels with him, then shall he sit upon the throne of his glory.

Matthews 25:31

Dedicated to
Greg and Cheryl Kreger
"Your love for the saints is
unassuming and strengthening,
while your worship of God, awesome."

Acknowledgments

The very demanding work on this book has been made possible and indeed enjoyable by the support and encouragement from my wife, Ann, and the anecdotal inquisitiveness of my daughters, Ednauh and Givean, and son, Fame. You added a great impetus to my efforts.

I am grateful to Jared Othieno Angira, who gave me useful suggestions on structural and editorial aspects of the work, and to my colleagues in the theological calling, who made valuable input to the debate on the subject; to the many friends who preferred to remain anonymous yet whose contributions were immensely invaluable to the success of this work; to Joan Mary Jackson, whose love and support has been unparalleled; to Jeff and Carmen Fisher, who have been a longtime support and source of inspiration; to Francis Mariga Gathenya, whose keenness on linguistic details helped me with various points of views, and to Gifty John who was among the first people to read the preliminary manuscript. To all of you who helped in one way or the other in making this work a success, I say thank you.

Lastly, I am grateful to God for his anointing and grace in the process of this writing, what has made it possible.

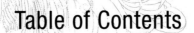

Table of Contents

Foreword

When I was first asked to read the manuscripts for this book, I thought, *Oh, not another book on angels*...but boy I was surprised! Silvanus' unique insight of angels vividly makes the subject alive and causes one to rethink their understanding of them. The book begins by defining the word *angel* and then biblically expounds on the characteristics of the cherubim, seraphim, archangels, and the other angels. My understanding of their individual beauty and "heart toward God" caused my heart to skip a beat and increased my desire to likewise please the Father in everything.

Throughout the Christian church's history, there have been many traditions on angels, some childish while others extremely complex. Silvanus addresses some of these traditions with challenging questions and brings "to the point" answers to each one while bringing clarity to the doctrine of angels using great biblical examples.

I promise you will find this book enlightening and fun; I was not able to put it down. It is refreshing and provides in simplicity a comprehensive understanding of angels and their relationship to God and mankind. I plan on it being my reference standard.

Luis Leon (Associate Technical Fellow, the Boeing Company)
New Heart Worship Center,
Seattle, Washington

Introduction

Angels are one of the biblical subjects that attract much attention, because people seem to be fascinated with them. Seemingly, over the world, almost in every culture and community people have some sort of angel stories. However, most people in general, including bible-believing Christians seem not to have complete and consistent information on them. That is where *Holy Angels, the Facts* comes in to help alleviate some of the ignorance within this subject area.

It was my desire to bring in a work that would clarify the many clouded viewpoints surrounding the origin, the role of and a number of factors concerning angels. *Holy Angels, the Facts* is my effort to concretize my commitment to fulfilling that desire. Written to simplify and amplify points of truth on holy angels, it is a quick-facts book for anyone desiring information on these heavenly beings. Yet it is challenging in its presentation and totally differs from the traditional teachings on angels in that it brings fresh perspectives to a host of areas.

For instance, even the term *angel* has been used

loosely and lost the weight of its real meaning with people attaching different connotations to it. As stated in a chapter below, some people call their girlfriends or spouses "angel," while to others, little babies are innocent angels; whereas, Mother Teresa, who worked among the poor of India, was called an angel of mercy and so forth. Nonetheless, *Holy Angels, the Facts* clearly restores the true meaning to the term *angel* bringing it out from its deep root word. It has broken away from the mystical and traditional classifications of angels based on the hierarchical tiers called choirs, and has classified them according to their positions in relation to God's personal presence. It vividly explains who the various angelic groups are, including clear differences between them. Eventually, it takes you to the question and answers chapter, dealing in depth with most frequently asked questions on angels.

I have endeavored in this work to present a viewpoint that is simple, yet biblically supported and having concrete details that lay credence to the doctrine as espoused in some of its areas. I trust you will find it informative and insightful, with the truth you gain from it demolishing the false understanding you might have held. Even those with no prior knowledge of angels will be informed accordingly.

It is important to state though that this denotation "angel" mainly applies to the angels deemed good or holy, for there are good and bad angels. The discussions in this work, therefore, relate mostly to the "good angels," those who remained loyal to God after the grand rebellion hatched and led by Lucifer. Those who went with Lucifer ceased to retain the designation "angels." Except mention may be made here and there of Lucifer or fallen angels, but that will be as sketchy as should be so we do not deviate from our specific study of the holy angels.

I hope your reading will be inspiring, enjoyable, and blessed.

Silvanus Oluoch

Part 1

Angel Defined

The word *angel* today means different things to different people. Some call their girlfriends or spouses "angel," while to others, little babies are innocent angels. Mother Teresa who worked among the poor of India was called an angel of mercy and so forth. Hence, there are varied meanings and connotations people attach to this term *angel*. But from the Scriptures it literally means "messenger," having been derived from the Greek word *aggelos* or *angelos*.

Studies show that the word *angelos* itself was derived from the Hebrew word *mal'akh*, which in its original root meaning was noted to mean "shadow side of God" or "God's shadow side." It was presumed to be the side or part (portion) of God that often but briefly appeared or showed itself to mankind. This arose from earlier connotations that God was invisible but occasionally allowed humans to see some parts of his being. It was held that whenever it pleased him, he often revealed that side to whomsoever he chose; hence, the reference *shadow side of God*.

However, as people developed in their understanding of God, they realized that *mal'akh* was not part of God but individual entities he sends to do his various biddings. In fact, the word *mal'akh* denotes someone sent over some distance to communicate a message. Hence, humans called them God's *messengers*, and that became their name. Moreover, that is how they are introduced to us, simply as angels (messengers); however, that term only depicts their functions rather than their nature or essence.

According to experts in both Hebrew and Greek languages, it is a word signifying a "messenger" and can be employed to denote human agents sent with or who carry certain messages to specific places or persons. But it is mostly used for non-human agents God sends forth or uses to execute his purposes. Examples of its usage referring to human agents are: "And there came a *messenger* unto Job, and said, The oxen were plowing, and the asses feeding beside them" (Job 1:14, emphasis added). "And the elders of Jabesh said unto him, Give us seven days' respite, that we may send *messengers* unto all the coasts of Israel: and then, if there be no man to save us, we will come out to thee" (1 Samuel 11:3, emphasis added). Other references: 1 Samuel 11:7, Luke 7:24; 9:51–52, Isaiah 42:19, Haggai 1:13, Malachi 2:7.

In the New Testament, it is used to also denote gospel ministers as in the book of Revelation. "The mystery of the seven stars which thou sawest in my right hand, and the seven golden candlesticks. The seven stars are the *angels* of the seven churches: and the seven candlesticks which thou sawest are the seven churches" (Revelation 1:20, emphasis added).

However, its distinctive meaning as pointed above is that which applies to the non-human heavenly intelligent beings whom God employs in carrying out his will as he deems necessary. This is the meaning we are going to concentrate on in our discourse in this book.

Thus, the word *angel* when applied to the celestial world simply refers to those heavenly beings with superhuman qualities, who stand ministering before God and wherever he wills. They are God's messengers, but in regard to who or what they are, the *appropriate* meaning would be ministers rather than just messengers. This is so because some angels are never sent from God's personal presence but serve in other capacities. They are called ministers in Psalm 104:4: "Who maketh his angels spirits; his *ministers* a flaming fire" (emphasis added). While in the book of Hebrews, they are referred to as ministering spirits, who minister to those who are heirs of salvation. "Are they not all *ministering spirits*, sent forth to *minister* for them who shall be heirs of salvation?" (Hebrews 1:14, emphasis added).

The denotation "angel" nowadays mainly applies to angels deemed good or holy, for there are good and bad angels. The Bible says when the Son of man shall come in his glory *and all the holy angels* with him, then shall he sit upon the throne of his glory (Matthews 25:31). The phrase "and all *the holy angels* with him" implies there are unholy angels.

The good or holy angels remained loyal to God when Lucifer staged a grand rebellion against him and led some away. Those who went with Lucifer ceased to retain the designation angel when they left their estate and are called the devil's angels. "Then shall he say also unto them on the left hand, Depart from me, ye cursed, into everlasting fire, prepared for *the devil and his angels*" (Matthew 25:41, emphasis added). They are the bad angels.

Angels' Nature

Angels are created beings, though in a different order of life from human beings. They are spirit beings residing in God's personal presence, though some of them are usually sent to minister away from that presence. They can appear in different forms to different people at different times as they are not limited by time and space. Their mode of travel seems to be instantaneous; they can disappear from one place and appear in another place thousands of miles away instantly. Different people have encountered them differently, sometimes even in dreams.

They are non-material beings who are not in any way human, though the earlier Roman Catholic traditions stated that they are made of fire-like fine *material* seemingly vaporous. But that was just a human viewpoint; angels are non-material beings. To be specific, they are spirit beings that only take the human form when appearing to humans. They sometimes have a brilliant radiation about them when appearing to the humans and their appearances are awesome, and in some instances they assure those they appear to not to be afraid (Matthew 28:3, Luke 24:4). They can take the human form and look more or less like people, but theirs is not a physical body. It is what scholars call anthropomorphism, which comes from Greek words: *anthropos,* meaning *man* and *morphe,* meaning *form.* It simply means *man form* or the form of man.

Hence, angels are not humans but take the human form when appearing to humans. By their biblical descriptions (the *cherubim and seraphim*, angels directly stationed in God's personal presence), they seem to be compound beings, though they never appear so on earth! They are not one thing, but compound in the sense that they have one face like a lion, an eagle and even human, all in one being. To us that is quite strange, yet that is the description we get of them from Ezekiel and Revelation. However, when they appear to humans, they usually take human form.

As a matter of fact, there are numerous scriptural records of angelic appearances to men: an angel appeared to and brought food to Prophet Elijah when he was faint and demoralized somewhere off in the Damascus wilderness.

> "And as he lay and slept under a juniper tree, behold, then an angel touched him, and said unto him, Arise and eat"
>
> 1 Kings 19:5

Another angel was sent to the Evangelist Philip as he held powerful revival campaigns in the city of Samaria. The angel told him to go south to the desert road running from Jerusalem to Gaza.

"And the angel of the Lord spake unto Philip, saying, Arise, and go toward the south unto the way that goeth down from Jerusalem unto Gaza, which is desert"

Acts 8:26

Philip obeyed and in the desert road met an Ethiopian eunuch, an important officer in the then Ethiopian government who had gone to worship God in Jerusalem.

"And he arose and went: and, behold, a man of Ethiopia, an eunuch of great authority under Candace queen of the Ethiopians, who had the charge of all her treasure, and had come to Jerusalem for to worship, Was returning, and sitting in his chariot read Isaiah the prophet"

Acts 8:27–28.

Philip then joined that officer in the chariot and helped him with the understanding of the portion of the book of Isaiah he was reading. (Refer to Acts 8:29–34). Using that opportunity, Philip gave him a full dose of the gospel, led him to the Lord Jesus Christ, and eventually water baptized him.

Then Philip opened his mouth, and began at the same Scripture, and preached unto him Jesus. And as they went on their way, they came unto a certain water: and the eunuch said, See, here is water; what doth hinder me to be baptized?

And Philip said, If thou believest with all thine heart, thou mayest. And he answered and said, I believe that Jesus Christ is the Son of God. And he commanded the chariot to stand still: and they went down both into the water, both Philip and the eunuch; and he baptized him.

Act 8:35–38

This transpired as a result of the angel's message to Philip, and there are many examples of angelic visitations we may not cite here. However, it is clear that in their appearances, angels take a bodily form like unto humans. But their own bodies are not physical ones of flesh and blood, neither are they glorified bodies. Moreover, they are not disembodied spirits either; they are just spirit beings. As spirit beings, they are non-material and are not limited by time and space. This means natural conditions are no problem or hindrances to them. They can walk right through walls and so forth.

They did not exist until God called them into being. However, their exact time of creation is not clear from the Scriptures. Some rabbinic writings suggest they must have been created on the second day, while others say on the fifth day, since it is when winged creatures flying above the earth were created. But those are just suggestions; however, it is possible they were created in eternity *past* before the Genesis account. (Eternity has no past; however, I have used the term *past* here to drive home the fact that angels were created in the very long ago, before there was measurable time.) Or it is possible they were even created in the Genesis 1:1 account, which states, "In the beginning God created the heaven and the earth."

There are those who hold that in the mention of the creation of these two expanses, heaven and earth, God did not go into details of everything that was in those realms then. Thus, in the creation of heaven, it must have been done complete with all that made it what it is including the angelic hosts therein. Hence, angels must have been created then at the beginning of the creative acts, whenever that was. But is it true that it was done by God calling them out into being by the creative power of his word.

> "Praise ye him, all his angels. Let them praise the name of the LORD: for he commanded, and they were created."
>
> Psalm 148:2, 5

The psalmist alludes that God commanded and they were created. He just spoke a word, and the angels came into existence. This seemingly was long before the earth and man were created. Some facts in the Scriptures point toward such a conclusion. Thus, it can be deduced that they existed long before the creation of the earth.

> "Where wast thou when I laid the foundations of the earth? When the morning stars sang together, and all the sons of God shouted for joy?"
>
> Job 38:4, 7

First of all, the references morning star and all the sons of God are usually understood as describing the same thing, though some people let them mean two different groups of beings. Nonetheless, they are referencing one and the same beings; the angels. Hence, when the earth's foundation was laid, angels were present and sang together for joy. This means they existed long before the creation of the earth, since they were witnesses to its foundations being laid.

They are also referred to in the above scripture as the morning stars. This has two-fold meaning. One, they are stars as they have a bright, shining splendor, what Psalm 104 calls "a flaming fire." The book of Revelation also calls them *stars*: "And his tail drew the third part of the stars of heaven, and did cast them to the earth" (Revelation 12:4).

Secondly, this reference, *stars* may be because of their innumerable numbers just like the stars of heaven. They are further referred to as *morning* stars, the word *morning* depicting their having come early or immediately after the dawn of creation just as morning, immediately follows dawn.

As to reference "sons of God," it is also found in Job 1. "Now there was a day when the sons of God came to present themselves before the LORD, and Satan came also among them" (Job 1:6).

This reference carries the sense that they had their origin or beginning from but not necessarily that they were born of God. Birthing and creating are two totally different acts. Angels were created by but not born of God. As used here, the term *sons of God* is *generic*, which in it widest sense means more than just male offspring. It means those of God's company or subjects including nations.

As earlier indicated, their movement is swift and instantaneous, and as God allows, they can assume any form to make their presence visible to the humans. But as spirit beings, they are not subject to death and all the deteriorating factors of human life; hence, they are classified as immortal. They are immortal but not eternal, since they had a beginning.

However, they are not in an earthly order of things with regard to life. That means their life's order is totally different from ours. They do not grow old, tired, and so forth. Life on earth is alien to their realm. Generally speaking, they are considered sexless, though often spoken of in masculine sense. However, they do not marry or propagate their kinds; their nature just does not cater for that. They are not related to each other in terms of family ties as each was independently created. They are not a race of beings but rather a company of spirit beings. They do not even seem to have personal interests or ambitions.

Angels Classified

Angels are in differing ranking orders, and within the church's traditional viewpoints, these have ranged from nine to twelve hierarchical levels; whereas, in the rabbinic teachings it was claimed that the classification was on four levels corresponding to the four divisions of Israel army as described in Numbers 2. However, according to Daniel 7:10, there are angels who attend or stand before God throughout while other scriptural references, teach that other angels also minister in various places away from God's throne. This then makes it clear that there are only two levels of angelic classifications.

1. Angels who minister constantly in God's personal presence
2. Angels who actively minister in and even away from God's personal presence.

These two groups are then also each further subdivided into two categories:

   a. The first one; "angels of the presence" are divided into Seraphim and Cherubim.

b. The second group; "angels that also function away from the presence," are the Archangel group and Gabriel-type angels.

Angels Constantly in God's Presence (Angels of His Presence)

The Seraphim

The literal meaning of this name is not exactly known but has been speculated to be a blend of the Hebrew words *Ser* meaning higher being and *raphim* deriving from *rapha*, meaning healer. Hence, they are thought to be beings of the higher realm whose presence or beings emanate health or healing to their surrounding. Others think that their name means (ser) *higher* and (raphim) *lively* or *living* beings or high lively or active beings; or simply, *highly active* beings, active in proclaiming God's holiness. They are considered the highest or first in rank among the angelic beings, who carry out what is called the throne ministry, having unparalleled attitude of exalted worship. They are always before God and never leave his personal presence. According to the Prophet Isaiah, they fly or hover above the throne of God crying holy, holy, holy. They are God's attendants with special purpose of proclaiming his holiness, as they are thought to be directly associated with his holy nature.

In the year that king Uzziah died I saw also the Lord sitting upon a throne, high and lifted up, and his train filled the temple. Above it stood the seraphims: each one had six wings with twain he covered his face, and with twain he covered his feet, and with twain he did fly. And one cried unto another, and said, Holy, holy, holy, is the LORD of hosts: the whole earth is full of his glory. And the posts of the door moved at the voice of him that cried, and the house was filled with smoke.

Isaiah 6:1–4

Traditionally, the name *seraphim* also means the burning or fiery ones, which implies they have a burning zeal for and rapturous devotion to God, totally given to his holiness. They are among the group of angels reportedly having wings. As a matter of fact, it is recorded they each have six wings in three pairs. They fly on two wings and use the rest to cover their legs and faces. This they do so they do not draw attention to themselves. They do not want to distract from the mystery and beauty of God's holiness.

The Cherubim

The word *cherubim* (*cherubim* is plural for cherub) has simply been defined as the order or ranks of angels, or angels in or of a certain order; though its proper root word has been at the center of uncertainty. Because of that, it has been made to mean different things by different people along its historical lines. It was suggested it means the fullness of knowledge, deriving from the phrase "full of wisdom and perfect in beauty" from Ezekiel in reference to Lucifer, or simply because they are filled with a knowledge which is the more perfect as they are allowed to behold the glory of God more closely. There is also the explanation that the word *cherub* originated from the Assyrian word *kirubu*, derived from *karâbu*, which means "to be near". It seems to be more relevant, for even in Kiswahili language, which has some roots and connection to the Arabic-Assyrian world, the word is *karibu*, meaning near or welcome.

Therefore, the relevant meaning of the word *cherubim* should be the *near ones*, always at God's personal presence, the familiar or personal servants of God seen as acquaintances or bodyguards. As such, it was used to refer to these heavenly beings that are so closely associated with God, paying him homage in service.

However, some Protestant scholars later advanced the theory that cherubim were just mere symbolic representation of some abstract ideas but were not exactly real. Such scholars brought more confusion than provided answers in unraveling the angelic mystery. Cherubim are real angelic beings in existence; they are not just symbolical representation of some abstract facts. There is no symbolism in the way the Bible describes them.

They first appeared in the Bible guarding the tree of life in Genesis and much later the Prophet Ezekiel first called them "Living creatures." He later perceived they were cherubim after he heard God speak to the man clothed in linen. The scriptures teach that they are on either side of God's throne.

"O Lᴏʀᴅ of Heaven's Armies, God of Israel, You are enthroned *between the mighty cherubim*! You alone are God of all the kingdoms of the earth. You alone created the heavens and the earth.

> Isaiah 37:16(ɴʟᴛ, emphasis added)

Hear us, O Shepherd of Israel, you who lead Joseph like a flock; you who *sit enthroned between the cherubim*, shine forth.

> Psalm 80:1(ɴɪᴠ, emphasis added)

Jehovah reigneth: let the peoples tremble. He sitteth *between the cherubim*: let the earth be moved.

> Psalm 99:1 (ᴅᴀʀʙʏ, emphasis added)

That is not all; it is also supposed that the Cherubim form and bear God's throne.

Then I looked, and, behold, in the firmament that was above the head of the cherubims there appeared over them as it were a sapphire stone, as the appearance of the likeness of a throne.

> Ezekiel 10:1

Connecting this to other scriptures, we get clear revelation of where and what God's throne is. It is not some dry dead old carving of wood or something, but a living being as everything about God seems to be alive! Ezekiel looked and beheld on the firmament above the cherubic wings, God's throne, which is upon the cherubim.

> He bowed the heavens also, and came down: and darkness was under his feet. And he *rode upon a cherub*, and did fly: yea, he did fly upon the wings of the wind.
>
> Psalm 18:9–10

It appears that God is so dependent on them that he might not even have a throne without them. Could this be what fooled Lucifer into rebellion? We do not exactly know, but we find cherubim positioned over things that directly and greatly concern God. Even, when Adam and Eve sinned in Eden and lost God's glory, it was the cherubim that were sent and positioned to guard the way of the tree of life.

As we have observed, the cherubim also reportedly have wings; in fact, some translations just refer to them as the winged creatures or winged ones.

> O Lord of armies, the God of Israel, seated *between the winged ones*, you only are the God of all the kingdoms of the earth; you have made heaven and earth.
>
> Isaiah 37:16 (BBE, emphasis added)

> Lᴏʀᴅ God All-Powerful of Israel, your throne
> is *above the winged creatures*. You created the
> heavens and the earth, and you alone rule the
> kingdoms of this world.
>
> Isaiah 37:16 (cᴇv, emphasis added)

This is reinforced by Ezekiel 10 verses five, eight
and nineteen:

> "And the sound of the cherubim's *wings* was
> heard even to the outer court. And there
> appeared in the cherubims the form of a man's
> hand under their *wings*. And the cherubims
> lifted up their *wings*, and mounted up from
> the earth in my sight"
>
> Ezekiel 10:5, 8 &19 (emphasis added).

> They each have four wings … and every one
> four wings; and the likeness of the hands of a
> man was under their wings.
>
> Ezekiel 10:21

Two of their wings are stretched downward while
two are stretched upwards until they meet the tips of
the wings of the other cherubim. The point where their
wings meet form what Ezekiel calls the "firmament"
upon which is the throne of God.

> And the likeness of the firmament upon the
> heads of the living creature was as the color of
> the terrible crystal, stretched forth over their

heads above. And under the firmament were their wings straight, the one toward the other: every one had two, which covered on this side, and every one had two, which covered on that side, their bodies.

Ezekiel 1:22–23

When God came down on Mount Sinai, the lightning and thick clouds usually associated with the cherubim were witnessed.

And it came to pass on the third day in the morning, that there were thunders and lightnings, and a thick cloud upon the mount, and the voice of the trumpet exceeding loud; so that all the people that was in the camp trembled. And mount Sinai was altogether on a smoke, because the LORD descended upon it in fire: and the smoke thereof ascended as the smoke of a furnace, and the whole mount quaked greatly.

Exodus 19: 16, 18

Thus, Cherubim seemingly accompany God everywhere as part of his entourage. They seem not to leave his personal presence, except for the ones positioned in Eden at the fall of Adam (man). While their counterpart the seraphim are related and dedicated to God's holiness, the cherubim are related to his throne and its functions. It has been supposed that they guard the throne, but I think it goes much further into the fact that they form it.

Ezekiel tells us they are Quadra-faced beings with multi-directional mobile capabilities, having wheels within wheels. Hence, it is implied that God's throne is portable and can be moved in any dimension and direction as he may wish. His movements, therefore, can be undertaken without turning or even negotiating a corner. Oh, what a mystery, but so is God!

Their images were put in various places in the Old Covenant:

a. Their images were put on the mercy seat according to Exodus 25:18–22. Mercy seat typified the throne of grace from where both grace and mercy flow toward humanity. This cherubic image on the mercy seat had the connotation that they minister right from, at, and to the very throne of God. Their image depicted the presence of the Almighty God.

b. Their image was also put on the veil (Exodus 26:31). This veil was a thick covering used to separate the holy place from the most holy; in fact, it concealed the most holy place. This depicted the cherubim's ministry in areas closed and unknown to the humans.

c. Their image was also put on the curtains (Exodus 36:8). Curtains represented their behind-the-scenes ministries, their unannounced or non-publicized ministry.

d. Their image was also in the temple, Solomon's (1 Kings 8:6–7). The Temple was the focal place of worship for the Jews then. It is where people gathered to meet with, sacrifice to, or hear from God then. Their image in the temple symbolized God's presence in the midst of his people, bringing his glory to the humans. This was because man had sinned and fell short of God's glory. God at that time symbolized his glory availed to the humans in the images of the cherubim in the temple. Temple as a place of worship, bearing their images means that their ministry in whatever form (forming the throne, upholding it, and so forth) is a focused form of worship to God. While the seraphim cry, "holy, holy, holy Lord God Almighty" and so on, the cherubim's just serve in silence, and that is part of their worship.

Cherubim is the class of angels Lucifer (Satan) belonged to before God selected and set him apart, exalting him seemingly above others. The Bible teaches that Satan was once a cherub. He was the anointed cherub—the cherub who had been set apart and elevated from the normal cherubic angelic ranks to a higher place, in God's placement for a special purpose in eternal affairs.

In fact, he was the only cherubim angel to be called the "anointed cherub." That might be the reason he has problems with Jesus the "anointed," but that for now is besides our focus. He was set upon the holy mountain of God where he walked up and down in the midst of the stones of fire. Even his name—Lucifer (son of the morning)—means one with bright splendor or the shining one. He had beauty, wisdom, and understanding at his disposal all to be employed in the worship and celebration of God. He even had unrestricted continuous access into the glorious personal presence of the Almighty God. He was perfect in all his ways until iniquity was found in him, when the unbridled pride of his own will led him to having his five famous "I wills."

> I will ascend into heaven
> I will exalt my throne above the stars of God
> I will also sit on the mount of the congregation
> I will ascend above the height of the cloud
> I will be like the Most High.

When iniquity was found in him, he lost his privileged place with God and even his designation, and he acquired a different name altogether. He now goes to and fro across the earth in a bid to recruit more rebels against God.

Angels Who Also Minister Away from God's Personal Presence

The Archangel Group (the Warriors)

This is the group of angels under the leadership of Michael the archangel. They have no specific name in the Scriptures, only referred to as "Michael and his angels." However, to distinguish them from others, the designation *archangel group* suits them, though some people just call this whole group the archangels.

But the word *archangel* as used in the Bible is in a singular form preceded by a definite article *the*, meaning it specifically applies to Michael alone. It simply means *chief* or *one above others*. Therefore, Michael the archangel seems to be the head of this group; he is in charge. However, from the sense of things, he is not the only one in this category of angels. It is true he is the only one the Bible specifically identifies as the archangel with references like, "Yet Michael the archangel" (Jude 1:9), but he is only a representative of and in fact the leader of this category of angels. The reference, *archangel Group* can help us see more than just Michael. Let's see how.

> But the prince of the kingdom of Persia withstood me one and twenty days: but, lo, Michael, one of the chief princes, came to help me; and I remained there with the kings of Persia.
>
> Daniel 10:13

The line "but, lo, Michael, one of the chief *princes*, came to help me" is what we are concerned with here. It indicates that among that group Michael was just one among many. This seems to confirm that in this category of angelic hosts, they are more than just Michael.

> And there was war in heaven: Michael and his angels fought against the dragon; and the dragon fought and his angels.
>
> Revelation 12:7

Michael and his angels fought against the dragon. This statement implies that Michael was in charge of a certain group of angels with which he engaged in this combat against the dragon. Michael seemed to have been a commander of sorts to that group of angels, bearing in mind this was a war situation. There is implication then that these must have been the warrior angels. And that is exactly who the archangel group is; they are the military wing of the angelic host, the heavenly holy warriors.

Jesus himself confirmed that there are military angels when he used a military term *legion* on the night of His arrest to refer to a certain group of them.

> And, behold, one of them which were with Jesus stretched out his hand, and drew his sword, and struck a servant of the high priest's, and smote off his ear. Then said Jesus unto him, Put up again thy sword into his place: for all they that take the sword shall perish with the sword.
> Thinkest thou that I cannot now pray to my Father, and he shall presently give me more than twelve *legions* of angels?
>
> Matthew 26:51–53 (emphasis added)

A Roman legion was made up of six thousand soldiers; this means Jesus was saying His Father could dispatch him seventy-two thousand warrior angels just at a request. However, this did not mean those were all the warrior angels there were with God. That was just a figure Jesus spoke of, but their exact numbers like the total of all angels is innumerable. But various schools of thought hold to different views in regard to their number. Some claim there are only seven archangels; others say there are only four and so forth. However, the Bible does not specify how many they are.

The fact remains that there are military angels, and because of the nature of their work, it requires they appear to be above others, not that they exactly are. As the authoritative enforcers of God's commands within the celestial realm, it is inevitable that they be seen to be above others if you understand how authority works.

It is implied in the scriptures that this Michael's group is on a level of their own from the other angelic categories. This means, they seem to be above the other groups, for the Bible refers to them as "chief princes" (Daniel 10:13).

However, this does not mean they are above others in superiority or power or anything, but seemingly in rank only. They are not more important than the rest but in accord with their function of keeping law and order within the celestial realm it is purposed they appear so. That means in God's placement order he has ranked them to appear above others; however with him, no one is more important than others; to him all are important as they complement each other. Hence, we should not look at their functional position from human standpoint and think others must be subordinate to them. No, in celestial realm that is not the case; everyone is important in their own specific functions, and all are subordinate to God alone. Whatever they do complements what others are doing.

The archangel group has an access to the throne room and to all the other areas of the created existence. That could be how they got around the throne and flushed out Lucifer and his evil team. They are the ones who put things in order as situations may call for within the celestial realm or anywhere else as in line with God's authority. Every rebellion to God's authority or confusion of any sorts to God's orders, they deal with sternly, except for the rebellion in man, which God himself is personally handling.

They are swift warriors under the command of their chief archangelic host, Archangel Michael, who himself functions under the most capable of all ever known commander in chief, Yahweh Sabbaoth, the *Lord* of hosts.

They are referred to as mighty angels (2 Thessalonians 1:7–8), able to take vengeance on those who have rejected the gospel of our Lord Jesus Christ in these present times. They are authoritative enforcers of God's dictates and commands.

The fact of warrior angels was also brought to light when the Assyrian king sent his armies to capture the servant of God, the Prophet Elisha who revealed to the king of Israel even bedchamber secrets of the Assyrian king. When that king learned about that, he sent his army to finish such a dangerous prophet. When his army came in a big convoy and surrounded the city of Dothan, the prophet's servant trembled at the sight of them. But Elisha asked God to lift the veil from his servant's eyes so he could see the mighty heavenly warriors, who were on their side. And God did it; Gehazi's eyes were opened, and he saw mountains full of horses and chariots all around. (Refer to 2 Kings 6:8–23.) The chariots were mostly associated with the king's soldiers.

Hence, when Gehazi was allowed to see chariots all round, he was shown the holy warriors of the King of kings. The fact that God has chariots is also confirmed in the scripture below.

> The *chariots* of God are twenty thousand, even thousands of angels: the Lord is among them, as in Sinai, in the holy place.
>
> Psalm 68:17 (emphasis added)

There is another account in the Bible when a heavenly personality was sent with a message to Daniel, and some wicked power in the heavenlies by the name Prince of Persia hindered him for a period of twenty-one days. It took Michael the archangel and his team to free him. I submit that this personality was none other than the Lord Jesus Christ himself, in His pre-incarnation. Let us look at the story closely.

> Then I lifted up mine eyes, and looked, and behold a certain man clothed in linen, whose loins were girded with fine gold of Uphaz: His body also was like the beryl, and his face as the appearance of lightning, and his eyes as lamps of fire, and his arms and his feet like in color to polished brass, and the voice of his words like the voice of a multitude.
>
> Daniel 10:5–6

Daniel looked and saw a man, not an angel clothed in fine linen. His loins were girded with the gold of

Uphaz. There is only one person who fits Daniel's description; to find out who he is, let us turn to the book of Revelation and hear another servant of God speak. This is the Apostle John the Revelator in the Isles of Patmos.

> I was in the Spirit on the Lord's day, and heard behind me a great voice, as of a trumpet, Saying, I am Alpha and Omega, the first and the last: and, What thou seest, write in a book, and send it unto the seven churches which are in Asia; unto Ephesus, and unto Smyrna, and unto Pergamos, and unto Thyatira, and unto Sardis, and unto Philadelphia, and unto Laodicea.
>
> And I turned to see the voice that spake with me. And being turned, I saw seven golden candlesticks; And in the midst of the seven candlesticks one like unto the Son of man, clothed with a garment down to the foot, and girt about the paps with a golden girdle.
>
> His head and his hairs were white like wool, as white as snow; and his eyes were as a flame of fire; And his feet like unto fine brass, as if they burned in a furnace; and his voice as the sound of many waters.
>
> And he had in his right hand seven stars: and out of his mouth went a sharp two-edged sword and his countenance was as the sun shineth in his strength. And when I saw him, I fell at his feet as dead. And he laid his right

hand upon me, saying unto me, Fear not; I am the first and the last.

Revelation 1:10–17

Let's compare the words of Daniel and John.

Daniel saw a *man*; John saw one like unto the Son of *man*. Daniel describing His apparel says he was dressed in fine linen with His loins *girded with the gold* of Uphaz. John says His garment went down to the foot and with *a golden girdle*. Daniel says His face was as the appearance of lightning and His eyes as lamps of fire, whereas John says His eyes *were* as a flame of fire. Daniel says His arms and feet were like in color to polished brass. John confirms this by saying His feet were like unto fine brass, as if they burned in a furnace. Daniel, describing His speech, says the voice of His words was like the voice of a multitude. John, on this, says His voice was like the sound of many waters.

Listen to Daniel's reaction when he saw all these: he says, "there remained no strength in me: for my comeliness was turned in me into corruption, and I retained no strength." Then go to John, who says, "I fell at his feet as dead." Then listen to how the man responded to Daniel. He said, "O man greatly beloved, fear not." And to John he also said, "Fear not."

It is clear that these two servants of God must be talking about the same person. The person had introduced himself to John as the first and the last, and we know him to be none other than our Lord Jesus Christ. In fact, if you read up to the end of that chapter, you will find this person standing alone, even above Michael the archangel.

> But I will show thee that which is noted in the Scripture of truth: and there is none that holdeth with me in these things, but Michael your prince.
>
> Daniel 10:21

If Michael was the commander of these warrior angels and this person was an angel somewhere in the angelic ranks, he could not refer to Michael the way he did. In talking to Daniel, he referred to Michael as *your prince*, excluding himself. This means, he was not subject to Michael and that he was of a higher rank than the archangel. However, following the heavenly protocol, we see that it was the archangel group with Michael in the lead who was released from heaven to go to His rescue.

In that account, Michael is specifically mentioned again by name. In military terms, during times of war, privates or sergeants are hardly mentioned, but the commander is referred to most of the times. This is the reason Michael's name is always at fore in any mention of the Archangel group, but he is not the only one in that group.

Nevertheless, whenever there is any kind of commotion in regard to resistance or rebellion, then the archangel group comes into force, with Michael in the lead. Yes, Michael and his angels (the group he leads) are warriors.

Gabriel-type Angels (the Messengers)

These are the ones people mostly encounter. They are the interactive ministering spirits carrying out God's orders and commands, fulfilling His purposes and displaying His majesty wherever they are sent. This is the way most of us know angels, as God's messengers. They are connected to God's great eternal redemptive purposes.

We have observed that a high profile angel, Michael the archangel was personally involved with helping Christ in His pre-incarnate appearing as mentioned in Daniel. Likewise, it is observable that another *high-profile* angel, Gabriel was sent to announce His incarnation. This Gabriel belongs to this messenger class of angels and probably may be the chief.

Therefore, this group we will refer to as the *Gabriel-type* angels. This is because Gabriel is not the only one in this group, who is usually sent far and wide from God's throne to carry out various duties. The Scriptures record how Gabriel was sent to Mary with a message about the coming Messiah through her. Some angels were even sent to announce the arrival of the Messiah to the shepherds on the day of His birth. It was an angel who told Joseph and Mary to flee into Egypt.

In fact, some remarkable persons, who brought about or marked the beginning of certain phases of God's dealings with humans, had their births announced by angels. Isaac's birth was announced one year before. Samson's birth was also announced to his mother.

And the angel of the LORD appeared unto the

woman, and said unto her, Behold now, thou art barren, and bearest not: but thou shalt conceive, and bear a son.

Judges 13:3

John the Baptizer's birth was also heralded by the angel Gabriel.

There was in the days of Herod, the king of Judea, a certain priest named Zacharias, of the course of Abijah: and his wife was of the daughters of Aaron, and her name was Elisabeth. And they had no child, because that Elisabeth was barren, and they both were now well stricken in years.
And there appeared unto him an angel of the Lord standing on the right side of the altar of incense. And when Zacharias saw him, he was troubled, and fear fell upon him. But the angel said unto him, Fear not, Zacharias: for thy prayer is heard; and thy wife Elisabeth shall bear thee a son, and thou shalt call his name John.

Luke 1:5, 7, 11–13

Then, a few months later, this very same angel (Gabriel) went to Nazareth to announce the proposed birth of Jesus to the Virgin Mary (Luke 1:26–31).

And in the sixth month the angel Gabriel was

sent from God unto a city of Galilee, named Nazareth, To a virgin espoused to a man whose name was Joseph, of the house of David; and the virgin's name was Mary.

And the angel came in unto her, and said, Hail, thou that art highly favored, the Lord is with thee: blessed art thou among women. And when she saw him, she was troubled at his saying, and cast in her mind what manner of salutation this should be.

And the angel said unto her, Fear not, Mary: for thou hast found favor with God. And, behold, thou shalt conceive in thy womb, and bring forth a son, and shalt call his name JESUS.

Luke 1:26–31

Characteristics of Angels

Angels have various characteristics including being referred to as mighty. But they are not Almighty, neither are they omnipotent, though some ancient mystery texts (Heikkaht, Zohar, and others) attributed most extraordinary and immense powers to them. But angels are only creatures and cannot do whatever they so desire or wish or even on their own go wherever they want. They only do God's bidding, going when and where he sends them.

Sometimes people think that angels just have the powers at their discretion to change into human forms whenever they so want. But that is not true both logically and even scripturally. Angels only took human form at God's appointed and specific missions; they just cannot do it at will! As created beings, they are limited by their nature, for they too have their own nature.

> For verily he took not on him the nature of angels; but he took on him the seed of Abraham.
>
> Hebrews 2:16

Jesus did not take on the nature of the angels. This confirms that angels have their own peculiar nature, which is neither human nor divine. Moreover, in every life sphere within the created existence, there is a gulf fixed between it and others that cannot be crossed. Molecular biology has discovered that organisms (creation) stay true to type. That simply means all created things keep within their fixed limitations, what science calls kingdoms: the animal kingdom, plant kingdom, and so forth.

It is impossible for animals to cross over from their respective kingdom into either the plant or even human kingdoms. It is impossible for a baobab tree to turn itself into an elephant regardless of how long it takes. It can be called any name, but in real life, it is just not true. Nothing can go beyond the limits God fixed for it. Nonetheless, mutation occurs but only within the same species: rose flowers remain rose flowers though they may acquire various colors. There is no time a rose flower will become a rattle snake! As such, it is difficult, rather impossible for an elephant to cross over into the human kingdom unless aided by God, and that is how it is even with crossing over from the angelic sphere to the human's or any other; it cannot be done at the angel's will.

It is impossible for angels to take human form at will, unless allowed by God and only for a specific purpose. This is so because God created everything for some specific purposes, and he set them in their respective spheres of life and only he can grant the power to change from one sphere into another. This means not even angels can take any form other than their angelic nature at will. They cannot change into humans at will. It is impossible; they cannot just do it.

Hebrews 2:16 mentioned that Jesus chose not to take the angels' nature. This raises the question as to the reason he did not take on the nature of the angels. This can be answered by the fact we have already mentioned that the order of life in the angelic realm is quite alien to ours.

> Because God's children are human beings—made of flesh and blood—the Son also became flesh and blood. For only as a human being could he die, and only by dying could he break the power of the devil, who had the power of death. Only in this way could he set free all who have lived their lives as slaves to the fear of dying.
> Therefore, it was necessary for him to be made in every respect like us, His brothers and sisters, so that he could be our merciful and faithful High Priest before God. Then he could offer a sacrifice that would take away the sins of the people.
>
> Hebrews 2:14–15, 17(NLT).

If Jesus were to have taken the angelic nature, he could not exactly be considered someone touched by the feelings of our infirmities. He wanted to wear the exact leather shoe mankind had. He needed to have a body like yours and mine that could feel pain and be affected by the natural calamities and elements. It is in it that he could have and share same human experiences and feelings, so that he might be a merciful high priest.

> So then, since we have a great High Priest who has entered heaven, Jesus the Son of God, let us hold firmly to what we believe. This High Priest of ours understands our weaknesses, for He faced all of the same testings we do, yet He did not sin. So let us come boldly to the throne of our gracious God. There we will receive His mercy, and we will find grace to help us when we need it most.
>
> Hebrews 4:14–16 (NLT).

Besides, angels do not seem to experience emotions like being merciful and so forth, though the Scriptures record that they rejoice at the rebirth of a sinner.

> Likewise, I say unto you, there is joy in the presence of the angels of God over one sinner that repenteth.
>
> Luke 15:10

However, my point is that angels are in a different plane or sphere of life from humans, and their lives are totally different. As human beings, we are subject to and limited by physical and natural laws; we are stuck within time and space while they are not. Nevertheless, they are not omnipresent; they can only be in one place at a time. God alone is omnipresent.

Angels express themselves in various ways displaying an array of characteristics. These include the fact that they are:

a. Obedient–especially to God in respect to their services.

b. Mighty–They are mighty but not almighty (Psalm 103:20). They excel in strength.

c. Wise and intelligent (2 Samuel 14:20)–Their intelligence is superior to humans', but they are not omniscience

d. Reverent–in worship and service

e. Faithful and dependable to fulfill their respective functions. You can depend on them to carry out their assignments.

f. Meek–do not harbor personal resentment (2 Peter 2:11), neither rail against their opponents (Jude 9).

g. Holy–they are set apart for and by God for His own purposes (Revelation 14:10, Matthew 25:31).

h. Straightforward–they deliver their message as is. They do not water the message down or get ashamed or compromise.

i. Good–Because they dwell in the presence of a good God, they exhibit goodness in their interaction with human beings.

j. Moral agents with free will and freedom of individuality–They posses the ability to think, make decisions and choices; for example, when

John wanted to worship an angel in the book of Revelation, the angels chose to remind him to worship God alone (Revelation 22:8–9).

k. Real but invisible to the human eyes–though occasionally may take human forms to appear to the humans.

These are beautiful characteristics that would transform any human societies if humans were all to respond to and embrace the transforming grace of God in Christ Jesus.

Angels' Functions

The angels' purpose is mainly God's service, which in relation to human beings is to:

1. Protect–The best example of this is seen in the life of Jesus when he was a baby.

"The angel of the Lord appeareth to Joseph in a dream, saying, Arise, and take the young child and his mother, and flee into Egypt."

Matthew 2:13b

2. Deliver or rescue–An example here is the story of Peter's rescue from Herod's jail according to the book of Acts.

About that time King Herod Agrippa began to persecute some believers in the church. He had the apostle James (John's brother) killed with a sword. When Herod saw how much this pleased the Jewish people, he also arrested Peter. (This took place during the Passover celebration.) Then he imprisoned him, placing him under the guard of four squads of four soldiers each. Herod intended to bring Peter out for public trial after the Passover. But while Peter was in prison, the church prayed very earnestly for him. The night before Peter was to be placed on trial, he was asleep, fastened with two chains between two soldiers. Others stood guard at the prison gate. Suddenly, there was a bright light in the cell, and an angel of the Lord stood before Peter. The angel struck him on the side to awaken him and said, "Quick! Get up!" And the chains fell off his wrists. Then the angel told him, "Get dressed and put on your sandals." And he did. "Now put on your coat and follow me," the angel ordered.

So Peter left the cell, following the angel. But all the time he thought it was a vision. He didn't realize it was actually happening. They passed the first and second guard posts and came to the iron gate leading to the city, and this opened for them all by itself. So they passed through and started walking down the street, and then the angel suddenly left him. Peter finally came to his senses. "It's really true!" he said. "The Lord has sent His angel and saved me from Herod and from what the Jewish leaders had planned to do to me!"

When he realized this, he went to the home of Mary, the mother of John Mark, where many were gathered for prayer.

Acts 12:1–12 (NLT)

There was also an earlier deliverance case still involving Peter.

There came also a multitude out of the cities round about unto Jerusalem, bringing sick folks, and them which were vexed with unclean spirits: and they were healed every one.

Then the high priest rose up, and all they that were with him, (which is the sect of the Sadducees,) and were filled with indignation, And laid their hands on the apostles, and put them in the common prison.

But the angel of the Lord by night opened the prison doors, and brought them forth, and said, Go, stand and speak in the temple to the people all the words of this life.

Acts 5:16- 20

Deliverance stories would not be complete without mentioning the story of Daniel in the den of lions (Daniel 6:15–23).

3. Bring or take messages, advice, or God's order to people–Cornelius, an Italian army officer, a high-ranking person for that matter though a gentile, was a worship-

per of the true God. He helped the Jews in many ways, even in building their worship places. God saw his heart yearning for a relationship with the Almighty and sent him an angel (Acts 10:1–8).

There is also the story of Evangelist Philip, who was holding revival meetings in the city of Samaria. But then an angel appeared to him with a new order as to the purposes of God for him. He was to leave that revival and go on a different mission away along the desert road to and from Jerusalem.

Then Philip went down to the city of Samaria, and preached Christ unto them. And the people with one accord gave heed unto those things which Philip spake, hearing and seeing the miracles which he did.
And the angel of the Lord spake unto Philip, saying, Arise, and go toward the south unto the way that goeth down from Jerusalem unto Gaza, which is desert. And he arose and went.

Act 8:5–6, 26–27a

Other examples: angels sent to Mary, Zacharias, and others.

4. Minister to those in hardship and or danger–The Apostle Paul was destined to appear before Caesar in Rome but was in danger of drowning at the sea. God in His omniscience knew about this and sent him an angel to give him a word of encouragement.

And now I exhort you to be of good cheer:
for there shall be no loss of any man's life
among you, but of the ship. For there stood
by me this night the angel of God, whose I
am, and whom I serve, Saying, Fear not, Paul;
thou must be brought before Caesar: and, lo,
God hath given thee all them that sail with
thee. Wherefore, sirs, be of good cheer: for
I believe God, that it shall be even as it was
told me.

Acts 27:22–25

The Prophet Elijah's story also comes to mind.
Greatly depressed to the point of death in the
wilderness of Damascus but an angel ministered to him, preparing him two meals and
refreshments, which energized and strength-
ened him for over one and half months.

(1 Kings 19:4–8)

5. Bring encouragements–This is illustrated by the story
of Gideon from Judges 6.

And the angel of the LORD appeared unto
him, and said unto him, The LORD is with
thee, thou mighty man of valor.

Judges 6:12

Paul also was encouraged by an angelic message.

For there stood by my side, last night, an angel of the God to whom I belong, and whom also I worship, and he said, "Dismiss all fear, Paul, for you must stand before Caesar; and God has granted you the lives of all who are sailing with you." Therefore, Sirs, take courage; for I believe God, and am convinced that things will happen exactly as I have been told.

Acts 27:23–25 (Weymouth)

6. Warn of God's judgment–God's angel clearly warned Abraham of the pending destruction of Sodom (Genesis 18:16–33). When Sodom was finally to go up in flames, angels warned and removed Lot from that city.

And when the morning arose, then the angels hastened Lot, saying, Arise, take thy wife, and thy two daughters, which are here; lest thou be consumed in the iniquity of the city.

Genesis 19:15

7. Execute God's judgment–Sodom's story exemplifies God's judgment (Genesis 19:1–29). There is also the execution of Egyptians' first born of both man and animals on the night of Israel's exodus (Exodus 12:29–36). From the New Testament, the story on God's angelic judgment is best exemplified by Herod, who allowed his people to worship him claiming he was God!

And Herod was highly displeased with them of Tyre and Sidon: but they came with one accord to him, and, having made Blastus the king's chamberlain their friend, desired peace; because their country was nourished by the king's country.

And upon a set day Herod, arrayed in royal apparel, sat upon his throne, and made an oration unto them. And the people gave a shout, saying, It is the voice of a god, and not of a man. *And immediately the angel of the Lord* smote him, because he gave not God the glory: and he was eaten of worms, and gave up the ghost.

Acts 12:20–23 (emphasis added)

8. Escort believers to their destination in God at death

And it came to pass, that the beggar died, and was carried by the angels into Abraham's bosom: the rich man also died, and was buried.

Luke 16:22

This beggar, called Lazarus, a name which meant "God has helped" or "whom God helps," stuck with God in his life on earth and it is recorded that he died and angels carried him to Abraham's bosom. The angels definitely had been directed by God and so they knew where to take him. Believers who hold on to God to the end should rejoice that God has angels instructed to direct them to their specific destinations in him.

Angels' Involvements in Human Life

In Jesus' Earthly life

Jesus came into this world and lived with the humans as one of them and eventually died for their redemption. His coming gave credibility and authenticated God's concerns and concept of human life. Being on earth as a human being, holy angels were actively involved in His earthly life right from birth, in fact even before conception to His ascension. He was aware and even anticipated angelic involvements with him when he clearly declared so to Nathaniel:

> And he saith unto him, Verily, verily, I say unto you, Hereafter ye shall see heaven open, and *the angels of God ascending and descending upon the Son of man.*
>
> John 1:51(emphasis added)

We have seen how angels were greatly involved in the annunciation, convincing Joseph not to boot Mary as he planned to secretly do.

Joseph was a man who always did what was right, but he did not want to disgrace Mary publicly; so he made plans to break the engagement privately. While he was thinking about this, an angel of the Lord appeared to him in a dream and said, "Joseph, descendant of David, do not be afraid to take Mary to be your wife. For it is by the Holy Spirit that she has conceived."

Matthew 1:19–20 (GNB)

Right from birth, angels were then constantly available to minister to him. In fact, it was an angel who instructed Joseph on the name "Jesus" to be given to the boy after birth.

She will have a son, and you will name him Jesus—because he will save his people from their sins.

Matthew 1:21 (GNB)

Angels even announced His birth to the Shepherds.

And there were in the same country shepherds abiding in the field, keeping watch over their flock by night. And, lo, the angel of the Lord came upon them, and the glory of the Lord shone round about them: and they were sore afraid.
And the angel said unto them, Fear not: for, behold, I bring you good tidings of great joy,

which shall be to all people. For unto you is born this day in the city of David a Savior, which is Christ the Lord.

Luke 2:8–11

An angel directed Jesus' family flight into and from Egypt when Herod secretly planned to execute the helpless baby with the rest of the kids two years and below in Bethlehem; that angel appeared to His parents and told them how and where to escape.

The angel of the Lord appeareth to Joseph in a dream, saying, Arise, and take the young child and his mother, and flee into Egypt, and be thou there until I bring thee word: for Herod will seek the young child to destroy him. When he arose, he took the young child and his mother by night, and departed into Egypt.

Matthew 2:13–14

Later on, angels ministered to him after His wilderness temptations and then in the garden of Gethsemane on the night of His arrest (Luke 22:43). On resurrection day, it was an angel who rolled the tomb stone away. And when Jesus ascended into the heaven, two angels appeared and spoke to His disciples. The Scriptures further say angels will be in His entourage when he comes again.

> For the Son of man shall come in the glory of
> his Father with his angels; and then he shall
> reward every man according to his works.
>
> Matthew 16:27

Hence, angels were remarkably involved in the life and ministry of Christ from the annunciation to ascension. This infers that his body, the church, which is still on earth, should also have angelic involvements in its ministry.

Human Interactions with Angels

Human beings do not have any scriptural basis for involvements with angels on their own terms, like commanding them, conversing with, and so forth. Unless the angels appear and begin talking to us, we are never instructed anywhere in the Bible to invoke their presence or appearance with a view to conversing with them or anything. Neither should we ask them questions about matters concerning us, our futures, and so on unless they are specifically sent with such orders. We are not to worship them or extol them in any way either; Paul implies that angel worship is one of the ways people lose their rewards:

> Let no man beguile you of your reward in a
> voluntary humility and worshiping of angels.
>
> Colossians 2:18

Angels like humans are creatures, who also worship and serve God. As a matter of fact, true angels will not accept human or any other worship. They all worship God alone and never accept to be worshipped.

> And I fell at his feet to worship him. And he said unto me, See thou do it not: I am thy fellow servant, and of thy brethren that have the testimony of Jesus: worship God.
>
> Revelation 19:10

(Read also Revelation 22:8–9.)

Angels in the Future

Angels will remain angels even in the future just as people will remain people. Human beings do not become angels at death or whenever they leave the earth. However, Origen, one of the church fathers, who converted to Christianity from heathen philosophy and Gnostics teachings, taught that men could become angels just as easily as angels can turn into men. He was responsible for views that provoked many contradictions during his lifetime, and even afterwards. But those were his personal views; they are untrue and unscriptural; people do not become angels.

Besides, some earlier rabbinic writings also claimed that the Hebrew patriarchs became angels on arriving to heaven. For example, tradition taught that Enoch after his translation became a god-angel referred to as Mal'akh ha-panin, also called Amshapands in some mystery religions. But that was just folklore meant to exhort people to virtuous living; it had no basis in the Scriptures.

However, borrowing from such notions, some people have taught that those who were or are virtuous in their earthly life become angels upon death. Others insinuate that their dead relatives either turn into angels or something, but those are thoughts borrowed from traditions contrary to the Holy Scriptures and hence, absolute errors. There is no scriptural or even logical basis for such unfounded extra biblical information. People remain people, and angels too remain angels; humans never transform into angels at any time.

1. Angels will be present when Jesus confesses before His Father the names of those who were not ashamed of him on earth.

   Also I say unto you, Whosoever shall confess me before men, him shall the Son of man also confess before the angels of God.

   Luke 12:8

2. They will appear with Christ when he comes again.

   And to you who are troubled rest with us, when the Lord Jesus shall be revealed from heaven with his mighty angels.

   2 Thessalonians 1:7

3. They will engage in the gathering of the elect at the end.

   And he shall send his angels with a great sound of a trumpet, and they shall gather together his elect from the four winds, from one end of heaven to the other."

   Matthew 24:31

And then shall he send his angels, and shall gather together his elect from the four winds, from the uttermost part of the earth to the uttermost part of heaven.

Mark 13:27

4. They will seal God's servants, the 144,000.

And I saw another angel ascending from the east, having the seal of the living God: and he cried with a loud voice to the four angels, to whom it was given to hurt the earth and the sea, Saying, Hurt not the earth, neither the sea, nor the trees, till we have sealed the servants of our God in their foreheads. And I heard the number of them which were sealed: and there were sealed a hundred and forty and four thousand of all the tribes of the children of Israel.

Revelation 7:2–4

5. An angel will bind the devil for one thousand years.

And I saw an angel come down from heaven, having the key of the bottomless pit and a great chain in his hand.

And he laid hold on the dragon, that old serpent, which is the Devil, and Satan, and bound him a thousand years,

And cast him into the bottomless pit, and shut him up, and set a seal upon him, that he should deceive the nations no more, till the thousand years should be fulfilled: and after that he must be loosed a little season.

Revelation 20:1–3

Personal Angelic Encounters

Personally, I have not had the privilege of seeing or encountering an angelic being, but my wife has; and I am going to relate one of her angelic encounters here for your information.

Angels Sent with a Word of Healing

This encounter occurred in a hospital ward when she had been diagnosed with a hole in the stomach, which the doctors thought she might have grown up with. One of them also suggested it might have been a result of an acid reflux that was not diagnosed and treated early enough. Whichever it was, she had a hole in her stomach.

I think it was just a case of different doctors saying different things. Our family doctor had diagnosed her with stomach ulcers, which we treated using the various prescriptions. But somehow she was not getting any better.

However, one time our family doctor was out of the country, and we opted for a different doctor, who carried out an endoscopic examination on her to find out the real problem. He also did some scans and X-rays, yet all those did not confirm the ulcers. This new doctor said he could not seem to find any ulcers, suggesting our family doctor might have misdiagnosed my wife's problem. According to him, my wife had no ulcers but could have been suffering from what he called dyspepsia. Also from one of the scanned images, the new doctor said my wife seemed to have gallstones in her liver, suffering from something he called cholecystitis. He recommended an immediate surgical attention.

This was arranged, and they did laparoscopic cholecystectomy whereby they cut out a piece of my wife's liver and gallbladder and purportedly removed the gallstones! But her situation did not change. We then arranged for her to go abroad for thorough examination and proper diagnosis and there her real problem was discovered. She returned home where we arranged for surgery to close the hole in her stomach.

When it was finally done, it took over six hours. The doctors on her case did their best; they cleaned the rot inside her and the bleeding, then closed the hole. They informed us that they thought it would be difficult for my wife to function normally again based on their experiences with such patients. In fact, they thought she would be paralyzed on her left side and would only move by the use of a wheelchair. They told us she would require total care throughout.

We were not allowed to see her immediately after the surgery until the following day on which I found her on every kind of tube: oxygen tubes, intravenous tubes, and others. She could not speak or open her eyes, but just laid there, swollen all over her body with tears coming out of the corners of her eyes.

However, by that evening she could open her eyes a little but could still not talk. She was still breathing through the artificial oxygen and being fed through the tubes. But suddenly her situation deteriorated and eventually she fell into a coma, which they told us she slipped into on and off. In one of those situations, the nurse called the doctor, who said that she would come out of that troubled time shortly and if she did not in a short while, they should call him again. It was then that something extraordinary happened in her life.

Somehow, she began seeing with her eyes closed; thus, she was not seeing earthly things but in the other realm. It was cinematic in its unfolding, and in its final stages two smartly dressed men appeared by her hospital bed and told her she was healed and did not need to lie there anymore. She, however, told them how that could not be true for she was in a lot of pain and was, in fact, in a hospital. She had not been able to talk since the operation, and this episode must have been in another realm also, for even none of her patient neighbors heard her say anything.

However, in her conversation with the two gentlemen, one of them told her they were angels sent from God to tell her she was healed and it was upon her to accept or decide what to do with their message. She immediately began laughing at how they seemed not to realize that she was not just slightly sick but had been operated on. That laugh was real and audible even in the hospital ward where she lay, though her conversations with the men had not been. While laughing she shook the various tubes on her mouth and nose, resulting in her patient colleagues thinking she was giving up the ghost, and they called a nurse urgently. (She was in a *four-people* shared ward). When the nurse came, she found her laughing and wondered what was exciting her, for she had been as a dead person. The nurse asked her what was up, to which my wife asked her, "Did you see them?"

"See them, who are they? What are you talking about?" asked the nurse.

"The two gentlemen who told me I am healed," responded my wife. She then went ahead and requested the nurse to remove the oxygen mask and the other tubes so she could tell them clearly. But the nurse was still puzzled; furthermore it was not yet even time for visitors to come into the wards. Where would the two men she was talking about have come from? Even none of her three neighbors saw anybody come or leave her bedside.

The nurse called in another nurse to help her, while in the meantime they had even called the doctor in charge of her case. My wife sat up in bed, and since she was receiving the drips, her sitting up stopped the dripping; and the nurse tried to position her well for it to continue. It was then that she clearly told the nurses her story and that she was healed. It was clear to them that something had happened to her, but they could not understand what it was.

When the doctor finally came, he said that sometimes patients' minds run and create every kind of pictures and images, especially what one may have been thinking about. He suggested that my wife must have been thinking much about being healed so her mind picked it up and began creating those images. But she insisted on what she had seen, telling them it was not just her mind; she was sure of it. They did not accept her explanations; and the doctor ordered she be left to relax, and her mind would return to normalcy. Nonetheless, she did not allow human reasoning to rob her of the certainty of her encounter with those angels.

By the following day, she was well and walking about all over the ward. For the first time in her days at the hospital, she used the bathroom by herself. She then requested to be discharged, but the doctor refused, claiming she was not able to eat solid food yet. The doctors had indicated that in normal operations, it would take from three to four days after surgery to leave the hospital, but by the fifth day she was still in hospital. However, on the sixth day, she was much better than the previous days; she could be fed from the mouth and occasionally breathed oxygen.

Nonetheless, she was discharged from the hospital after eight days. She accepted her healing from God, through those angelic messengers and never got paralyzed on her left side, neither did she get confined to a wheelchair as the doctors had predicted. She has been walking on her own and even works ever since she left the hospital; she was totally healed.

From this encounter, it is deducible that these angels or people who appeared to my wife did not have wings as some people would associate with angels. They were just like ordinary people. Sometimes angels just appear as regular people, the reason the Bible tells us:

> Be not forgetful to entertain strangers: for thereby some have entertained angels unawares.
>
> Hebrews 13:2

Part 2

Some Common Questions on Holy Angels Answered

1. *Are angels better to God than human beings, since there is a scripture that says man was made slightly lower than angels? In what aspects is man lower than the angels?*

Answer: The issue of which of these two categories of created intelligent beings is better to God than the other does not even arise. Each of these categories of beings has their unique place, value, and worth before God. He does not contrast between and compare them as to which is more valuable than the other; each has its own order and purpose in creation. Angels, as we have pointed out or mentioned above, are of a different and in fact a higher order or realm than the human earthly life. But that does not mean they are better or of more value to God than the humans. It is only that they were created and suited for that realm, to be at God's disposal for service, while man was brought here to be the mirror image of God, while exerting dominion on the earth.

God made man in His image and likeness so man

may interact with God in fellowship and worship, by which man is to partake of God's divine nature. Man at that point was to reflect or radiate God's glory on earth. He was given the honor to reflect the glorious God to all the created existence on the earthly realm. However, he failed on this when he sold out to the devil. Man fell short of God's glory; nevertheless, God did not give up on man. He is not through with man as far as that eternal purpose is concerned. Therefore, we clearly see that each of these two groups, angels and humans, have their respective places and functions in God's eternal purpose that is not competitive or comparable.

However, when we consider the fact that man was honored to bear God's image on earth, and was given dominion in a whole realm like the earth; was allowed opportunity of relating with God in family arrangements and even allowed free communion, communication, and fellowship; he was given the privilege of and option for redemption when he fell, what fallen angels do not have. Add to the fact that as a member of God's family, man has the honor to be God's heir, in fact, joint heir with Christ. He also has the privilege of being God indwelt and more. Therefore, with such reasons, one may be tempted to think that man then is better to God than angels. But that is not the case!

Because were it possible or permissible for angels to compare themselves to humans, they would also have felt like they are better to God than humans. This could be because God spared them the harrowing experiences of the human earthly life with all its limitations and degenerative aspects, i.e., growing old, getting tired, getting sick, hurt, dying, and so on. They have a full access to God's very presence, the privileges of living by direct contact with him, living within His realm. They do not have to live by faith; they are not bound or limited by time and space.

However, it is clear angels will not and cannot compare themselves to humans as this would be casting shadows on God's creations wonderfully and fearfully made. In other words, it would be like telling God he created beings of lower nature and lesser value than themselves. That would be pitting themselves against God, and that they just cannot do.

Anyway, it is a fact that with God none of these groups of being is better than the other; they were all created for His pleasure and for different functions within his eternal plans. As long as they serve His purposes, they are all equally important to him, though some rabbinic texts ranked man above angels. But we cannot simply use our human reasoning and decide which of these two is more important to God. He has not specifically said any of them is, so it is safe to trust that they all are.

Coming to the second part of this question, I think we need to quote those verses of scriptures here.

> What is man, that thou art mindful of him? and the son of man, that thou visitest him? For thou hast made him a little lower than the angels, and hast crowned him with glory and honor. Thou madest him to have dominion over the works of thy hands; thou hast put all things under his feet.
>
> Psalm 8:4–6

These verses have a dual application. First they are talking about our Lord Jesus as a person, who was made slightly lower than angels when he took on human form through incarnation. Second, they talk of man in general, who was made to have dominion over the whole earth but lost it by the fall. We can then say that man is lower than angels but only in respect to his current position and station. Yet man will not always be lower than angels. When God completes His redemptive and salvific work, man will occupy that place of dominion designed for him from the beginning. He will rule together with Christ being joint heir, with angels at their disposal. In fact, man will judge angels. Paul asks,

> Know ye not that we shall judge angels? how much more things that pertain to this life?
>
> 1 Corinthians 6:3

The nature of this judgment is not clearly expressed at the moment, but the Bible says man shall do it. It might turn out to be a judgment on the performance of their services, or even as is mostly held; a judgment upon the fallen angels. It would likely be bringing them to face the results of the reality of all they did against God's purpose for and in humanity. Man who was the victim of their perversion and rebellion against God's ordained life and purposes will be their judge. Man as a victim will be the clear presentation of the reality of God's good life intended for the creation, yet perverted and fought against by those fallen angels.

Therefore, at the culmination of God's redemptive acts, none of God's creation will be in any lower level so to say. Everything will be lifted to their respective intended positions before the dawn of their creation. As I have mentioned, man will rule and reign with Christ on His throne of authority with angels at their disposal.

2. *What is the angels' relationship to God? We know humans (Christians) call God our Father who is in heaven. Being in heaven do angels also call him Father?*

Answer: We will begin addressing this question by answering the angels' relationship to God. Angels relate to God on the basis of Creator/creature or Master/servant. They cannot and do not call God Father as there is no human family-type relationship between them other than being a community in God's heaven. There are no family ties binding them to God. He did not give birth to or bear them.

> For unto which of the angels said he at any time, Thou art my son, this day have I begotten thee? And again, I will be to him a Father, and he shall be to me a Son?
>
> Hebrews 1:5

The New American Standard Bible reads,

> For to which of the angels did He ever say, "THOU ART MY SON TODAY HAVE I BEGOTTEN THEE"? And again, I WILL

BE A FATHER TO HIM, AND HE SHALL
BE A SON TO ME."

Hebrews 1:5 (NASB)

God brought angels into existence only through creation, and they became a community of celestial beings but not along family lines. It is a known fact that communities can be formed even by people who are not blood related.

However, man gets the privilege to be in God's family through the second birth. The first birth ushers people into the human family, while the second birth ushers them into God's. Jesus told Nicodemus, "Verily, verily, I say unto thee, Except a man be born again, he cannot see the kingdom of God" (John 3:3). And John adds that, "But as many as received him, to them gave he power to become the sons of God, even to them that believe on his name" (John 1:12).

Jesus, who became the true mediator between God and man, shed His blood for this same purpose, the birthing of man into God's family. Therefore, it is on the basis of this blood relationship that man received the Spirit of adoption, whereby we cry, "Abba, Father." Angels are not indwelt by this Spirit and hence, cannot cry or say "Abba, Father." They do not have the privilege of being born again, in fact even being born once, for they were never born in the first place.

Nonetheless, God has been depicted in a number of ways throughout human history: the two major depictions being as a husband and a father. The former was mostly in the Old Testament where God was depicted as a husband to Israel, implying he was Israel's provider, protector and establisher. The term also carried the thought of being in deep and mutual committed relationship to one above others. A husband is supposed and should be committed to only one wife at a time. The husband depiction showed God as committed to Israel alone, and she too was supposed to do the same.

Nonetheless, that depiction as a husband had its own limitations as it was restrictive; it was just God and Israel and no other race. But God in Jesus Christ was reconciling the whole world to himself, so a restrictive metaphor could not then be applied to him. God was instituting a new thing in the earth then, not limited to a select few but to as many as would believe and trust him.

Hence, in the New Testament the depiction husband is not used for God though the book of Ephesians uses the terms *husband* and *wife* and the book of Revelation talks of the bride and the bridegroom, but within a different context.

Instead, in the New Testament, God is now portrayed with another relational depiction, that of a *Father*, though also used in the Old Testament to refer to him; especially the Prophet Jeremiah used it a lot. But it was not a major depiction then. It was mostly used when petitioning God or reminding people of their common destiny deriving from him. It was a way of trying to evoke their closeness and origin of their relationships with him whenever they found themselves in some predicaments. However, even God himself assumed it in referring to Israel.

> They shall come with weeping, and with supplications will I lead them: I will cause them to walk by the rivers of waters in a straight way, wherein they shall not stumble: for *I am a father* to Israel, and Ephraim is my firstborn.
>
> Jeremiah 31:9 (emphasis added)

Moreover, in the following Scripture the Israelites also refer to God as their father.

> As cattle are led into a fertile valley, so the LORD gave his people rest. He led his people and brought honor to his name. LORD, look upon us from heaven, where you live in your holiness and glory. Where is your great concern for us? Where is your power? Where are your love and compassion? Do not ignore us. *You are our father.* Our ancestors Abraham and Jacob do not acknowledge us, but you, LORD, are *our father*, the one who has always rescued us.
>
> Isaiah 63:14–16 (GNB, emphasis added)

> But *you are our father*, LORD. We are like clay, and you are like the potter. You created us, so do not be too angry with us or hold our sins against us forever. We are your people; be merciful to us.
>
> Isaiah 64:8 (GNB, emphasis added)

(See also Deuteronomy 32:3–6, Malachi 2:10.)

However, this depiction "father" was more fitting for use in the New Testament as it was the most universally accommodative depiction of God to as many people as would come to him by faith, regardless of their race, color, or geographical locations. God was no longer portrayed as a husband figure but rather a father to whosoever wills.

These terms, *husband* and *father*, are just human terms of designation for describing God, who is in no way human. It is what theologians call anthropomorphism, which is simply depicting God in human language or terms involving even attributes and characteristics. In fact, there are several passages in the Bible that ascribe to God human actions, attributes, and emotions, for he works with humans to bring about His sovereign will and purpose within their time and space frame.

But in reality, God is purely God.

> Know therefore this day, and consider it in thine heart, that the LORD he is God in heaven above, and upon the earth beneath: there is none else.
>
> Deuteronomy 4:39

The Scriptures clearly teach that *the* LORD *he is God in heaven above* not a Father, which we have observed to be an earthly title or term. When Jesus speaks (in Matthew 23:9) about us having a Father in heaven, he is speaking from an earthly viewpoint. For in fact, it is Jesus who introduced the usage of the term *father* in referencing God while here on earth to show us or depict

His relationship with him. That was so because, as has been said, the historical Jesus lived at a certain point in time, in a certain place among a certain people within a certain cultural and social context. Hence, His references to God as father were historically conditioned as an essential way of communicating about God.

Thus, *father* was and is an earthly term that does not apply to God in heaven, for from the heaven's perspective God is just God.

> Know therefore this day, and consider it in thine heart, that the LORD he is God in heaven above, and upon the earth beneath: there is none else.
>
> Deuteronomy 4:39

> Hear, my people, and I will speak; O Israel, and I will testify unto thee: I am God, thy God.
>
> Psalm 50:7 (DARBY)

God is God in heaven, though on earth humans refer to him as Father, but he is not a gender being, male or female. No wonder, John says, "For God so loved the world, that he gave his only begotten Son, that whosoever believeth in him should not perish, but have everlasting life" (John 3:16).

That verse does not read, "For the Father" so loved the world, but says God so loved. Since God loved the world and gave His Son—from the human perspective this connotes that there was an existing and a continuing relationship between the two. And as the sent one is the Son, then generally the understanding was that the sender must of necessity have been the Father.

The Hebrews placed great importance on fatherhood and accorded fathers honor and absolute authority as heads of their family units. It is said that "Father" in respect to their understanding came to be a title of honor and authority. Thus, they had no other understanding in regard to a son relating to another person to the point of being sent by him other than that of a father and a son. Hence, the term *father* found its culmination in this relationship between Jesus on earth and God in heaven portraying a close and personal relationship, which in human terms was a familial one. It was meant to portray that God is an intimate God, full of love and understanding.

Hence, Jesus used this term *father* from the human standpoint for ease of the humans grasping the fact of an existing relationship within the Godhead. Furthermore, since Jesus was into the mission of establishing a relationship between God and the humans; the title father was to make it easy for them to conceive and understand him as the authority in the relationship they were to enter into with him. God was to be personal to them not some abstract god like the idols that people made and called god. Hence, God for the humans became or was understood to be Father, but he is not Father; that is just a human designation.

Nonetheless, scriptural studies show that it is God who had promised in the long ago through His prophet that he would be a father to Jesus: "I will be his father, and he shall be my son" (1 Chronicles 17:13).

The scripture above is cross-referenced to Luke 1: 32–33. In its appearance in 1 Chronicles, it has a dual application. It is referring to Solomon and to the greater than Solomon, the Lord Jesus Christ who is known to have promised to build his church; a house for God's name (Matthew 16:18 and 2 Samuel 7:13).

Thus, it is God who had promised the application of the term *father* to His relationship with Jesus while here on earth and inherently to the many sons who were to follow Jesus. Therefore, when he finally came, Jesus brought the use of that term *father* to the fore by referring to God as His Father on several occasions and even teaching His disciples to refer to God as their Father which art in heaven. He even directly taught that we have a Father in heaven.

> And call no man your father upon the earth:
> for one is your Father, which is in heaven."
>
> Matthew 23:9

But all that was from an earthly or human stand-point depicted in the relationship between David and Solomon from which God was drawing the parallel.

Thus, when Christians refer to God as Father, definitely they do not mean some tall or short person living in time and space. It is true they are not talking of an earthly figure, but in their minds some of the attributes of the earthly person may be conceived in their conception of God's being, though God is not any of that. Their meaning is of necessity different, because as has been said, human language about God is not literally true. Even when Adam and Even heard the voice of God walking in Eden; it is not literal that God came walking down on two feet. That is employing human language to express things about God, but human words mean something different in human plane compared to the reality they refer to in God's realm.

This term *father* also signified that God is the one from whom all things spring, and it depicted him well to the humans. Fathers are understood or known as the ones from whom others spring; in most cases they are the source of many things within human families.

> But to us there is but one God, the Father, of whom are all things, and we in him; and one Lord Jesus Christ, by whom are all things, and we by him.
>
> 1 Corinthians 8:6

The amplified Bible reads:

> Yet for us there is [*only*] one God, the Father, *Who is the Source of all things* and for Whom we [*have life*], and one Lord, Jesus Christ, through and by Whom are all things and through and by Whom we [*ourselves exist*]. [*Mal.* 2:10.]
>
> 1 Corinthians 8:6 (AMP)

Hence, *father* is a human term that is foreign to the celestial realm, and as such, angels do not call God or address him so.

3. *You have stated that angels are sexless, neither male nor female, yet there are some teachings that purport Gabriel to be a female angel. What do you say to this?*

Answer: Sometimes people come up with such strange ideas convinced they are right, but they are not for they are contrary to the very order of things in God's revelation to mankind. Most of such people have been influenced by the feminine agitations arising from feminine movements that have complained at the way everything in the Bible to them is dominated by male portrayal and actions. No wonder, we have even heard them coin in terms like *Mother*-Father God. Such people always try introducing the feminine aspect into everything; nonetheless, much of such attitudes spring from the Gnostic teachings of the earlier centuries that were themselves continuation of some of the olden mystery cults involved in the worship of among others, the Queen of heaven.

> Seest thou not what they do in the cities of Judah and in the streets of Jerusalem? The children gather wood, and the fathers kindle the fire, and the women knead their dough, to make cakes to the queen of heaven, and to pour out drink offerings unto other gods, that they may provoke me to anger.
>
> Jeremiah 7:17–18

This worship was of a licentious character common among the heathen nations like the Moabites and the Midianites and many others. It was an organized religion involved in with much ceremony.

One commentator says that their idolatrous respects were paid to the *queen of heaven,* the moon, either in an *image* or in the original, or both. They worshipped it probably under various names; like in Baal worship, the female goddess was called Asherah and Venus in other places. The fact is that they always had some feminine aspects to their gods. This form of worship, despite the rising of Christianity with power and grace, still progressed even into the New Testament times, where in places like Ephesus it was the worship of goddess Diana.

> Moreover ye see and hear, that not alone at Ephesus, but almost throughout all Asia, this Paul hath persuaded and turned away much people, saying that they be no gods, which are made with hands: So that not only this our craft is in danger to be set at naught; but also that the temple of the great goddess Diana should be despised, and her magnificence should be destroyed, whom all Asia and the world worshippeth. And when they heard these sayings, they were full of wrath, and cried out, saying, Great is Diana of the Ephesians.
>
> Acts 19:26–28

Such Gnostic teachings did not end then; they are being propagated even today though in their modern forms clothed in Christian garb and are very subtly introduced even into a number of Christian circles without being suspected. But it is always about the feminine aspect of God, angels, earth, and so forth. In fact, currently most people have heard the phrase *mother-earth* commonly being peddled around.

Nonetheless, the claims that Gabriel is a female angel is just a logical deduction such folks arrive at from their skewed study of the Bible. One of their arguments claims that since Gabriel was associated with many conceptions and births then *he* must be female. But that is a simplistic reasoning that would have us believe that the male doctors and nurses who deliver women in labor wards are all female! Just because one is found or associated with the birth of children does not turn them into a woman, if they were not in the first place. You do not have to be a woman to work in a labor ward or be associated with childbirth!

They also claim that Mary would have not freely spoken to Gabriel if he was a man, especially a stranger in Galilee. The claim is based on the Hebraic traditions of morality and virtuous living that barred Hebrew girls unaccompanied from speaking to strange men. Thus, since Mary just got easily into a conversation with Gabriel, they claim he must have been a fellow woman for Mary to be that free. Nonetheless, that is just a logical derivation they are trying to arrive at so as to justify their stand, but there is no truth in it. I believe it was the awe of Gabriel's appearance and his approach what made Mary not think in Hebraic terms and responded to him uninhibited. He just happened to appear from nowhere and before she could think, Gabriel greeted her.

The angel greeted Mary and said, You are truly blessed! The Lord is with you.

Luke 1:28 (CEV)

But she, seeing the angel, was troubled at his word, and reasoned in her mind what this salutation might be.

Luke 1:29 (DARBY)

Then the angel told Mary, Don't be afraid! God is pleased with you.

Luke 1:30 (CEV)

The angel began by telling her good things about herself: *you are truly blessed! The Lord is with you*. In that state, she did not have time to think whether to talk to him or not. She must have wanted to hear more about the Lord who was pleased with her. The angel's tact engaged her so wonderfully in the conversation that she could not help but find herself conversing with him. Where she could have feared, the angel calmed her fears giving her assurance by invoking the name of God, and that settled it all.

However, looking closely at the Scriptures, we can see that Gabriel is not a female angel (there is nothing like a female angel), for the Bible clearly refers to him as a *he*.

And I heard a man's voice between the banks of Ulai, which called, and said, Gabriel, make this man to understand the vision. So he came near where I stood: and when he came, I was afraid, and fell upon my face: but he said unto me, Understand, O son of man: for at the time of the end shall be the vision. Now as he was speaking with me, I was in a deep sleep on my face toward the ground: but he touched me, and set me upright.

Daniel 8:16–18

Furthermore, in Daniel chapter 9, the Bible plainly refers to him as the *man* Gabriel.

Yea, while I was speaking in prayer, even the man Gabriel, whom I had seen in the vision at the beginning, being caused to fly swiftly, touched me about the time of the evening oblation.

Daniel 9:21

How is he female when the Bible clearly calls him "the man Gabriel"? Why can't people just stick with and simply believe the Bible? It is only those who do not want to believe the simplicity of the Bible that try to create their own understanding in such matters, much more what they want. However, strictly speaking, Gabriel is neither male nor female even though he is spoken of in male terms; he is purely an angel.

4. *How about the teaching that during Noah's time some angels came down to earth and married the daughters of men, how true is it?*

Answer: This teaching began small but has had some inroads into the wider Christian circles and is now propagated by and believed by many Christians worldwide. Divisive debates have raged over it as it is a controversial teaching, pitting some eminent theologians and respected Christian scholars and personalities from both sides of the divide. Hence, in regard to it, there are two major schools of thought; those pro and those against. My views here present one side of the arguments in the latter category. Thus, in response I will be referring to it as *angel-marriage* teaching or to those who teach it as angel-marriage teachers.

Amazingly, even most books on angels treat it so unsatisfactorily because people seem not to want to appear controversial; some do it as a passing notice. Nonetheless, we will face it here and scrutinize some of its major points to see how they measure against the Scriptures. Some of the major points are:

a. The very basis of the teaching

b. Implications that angels can change form at will

c. Claims that angels came to earth and married women

d. Creature functioning outside of God's design

e. The phrase "sons of God"

f. Major scriptures used in support of that teaching.

The Very Basis of the Teaching

This teaching does not fully correspond to the whole

counsel of God's Word from the outset. It carries some elements of good reasoning but which are totally lacking true biblical revelation, as far as angelic beings are concerned. Its propagation is based on presumptuous interpretations that do not stand the true test of God's Word. It was built on the purported understanding of the words *sons of* God purely *based on the Jewish earlier understanding of that expression.*

But those same Hebrews also held then that angels were recreated daily through God's every breath as a band to sing before him and then perish the same day. Yet, those who borrowed the phrase *sons of God* from them do not hold to that understanding today. Why? Simply because that is not true to the current knowledge and understanding of angels; angels do not die or expire daily.

This teaching is mostly derived from mythology and other literatures (apocryphal and pseudepigraphical), especially the book of Enoch, which though informative are extra biblical and should not form our basis of understanding biblical facts. But some folks keenly read such literature and then borrow wholesale ideas from them and then look for scriptures to support their newfound knowledge; doing that even though some of such materials are contradictory to the Bible.

Not every literature talking about angels is scripturally sound. Experts in this area have averred that in those literatures the angelic teaching turned so bizarre and left the impression of the unbridled religious imaginations then. But even today imagination has not waned, and there is much talk about angels, even with movies being made about them. But most of such efforts have incorporated so much unscriptural material sources and notions that believers should not rely on them for facts about biblical angels. *Christians, beware; do not get your facts from movies.*

Nonetheless, the proponents of angel-marriage teaching have tried to make it *true logically*, but it is scripturally false to *the spirit and letter* of God's Word. It has heavily borrowed much from non-biblical sources as mentioned above. Its very basis is wrong.

Implications that Angels Can Change Form at Will

Considering the very nature of angels, it is impossible for any of them to change at will into another state. But the angel-marriage teachings argue that if the holy angels can appear as human beings and participate in some human activities like eating, then even the fallen *angels at one time must have done so and engaged in such evil deeds.* However, that is a presupposition that cannot be substantiated.

The change angels usually undergo to appear to the humans is always sanctioned by God; it is not anything of their own doing. That is the reason it is mind boggling how those purported "sons of God" could have changed into men to come and marry the daughters of men without God allowing or even aiding them to change! It is contrary to the revealed way of how God operates. But the proponents of this doctrine talk as if angels just have the power inherent within them to change into humans, whenever and wherever they so wish. Yet that is totally false to scriptural revelation!

Just as humans cannot change from human sphere to any other, even angels as created agents cannot do so either. For every species to function on planes not their own there has to be a reconstitution of their structural frames and capabilities. That is the reason we are currently partaking of the divine nature so that we could be fitted for the life in the celestial realm. And the Apostle Paul intimates that we shall all be changed in the twinkling of an eye. This means we shall undergo a total change.

Likewise, for every species to function in a different realm, they must be reconstituted to be compatible with the new realm's life. This means even for the angels to function in the lower human plane they need a reconstitution, which God alone could do or allow! As such, the angels who allegedly came to earth to live the human life needed God to reconstitute them; yet, it is difficult to believe God did that.

The irony of this teaching is the presumption that those angels took upon them not only human form but even the very nature, which then gave them the abilities to function fully as human beings! But from scriptural references, it is clear that angels only take human forms when appearing to people on earth with a specific mission from God. It is just a form they take on, an image and only a vehicle for message delivery. When they are through with their mission, they immediately disappear back into their realm.

For any being to acquire the very nature of man, they must be born into the human race taking after Adam! Yet, that is *a creative act* that only God can affect. Even

Jesus himself (the creator) did not undertake the taking of human nature by just descending or appearing down here from heaven. He opted for the right way, the birth doorway so as to become a real human. It is important to understand this; to be human one must be born into the human race. Therefore, for those so-called angels to have been humans, they needed to have been born into the human race, which was not the case. It is, therefore, false to deduce that they came down to earth and functioned as humans even marrying.

Others within the proponents of this teaching have also taught that the angels who came and cohabited with women on earth were of a separate rank and order, more near to the humans in nature, genes, and sexual enthusiasm, for they were also called sons, which is a human term. But where do they get such reasoning from? Does the Bible say there are two or three or different kinds of angelic nature? It does not; thus, such reasoning is just human efforts at explaining things that do not add up in their presentation of their story.

Claims that angels came to earth and married women

The Bible clearly states: "For in the resurrection they neither marry, nor are given in marriage, but are as the angels of God in heaven" (Matthew 22:30).

This is in the authority of none other than Jesus Christ himself who said that angels neither marry nor are given in marriage. But then why do some people through human logical reasoning and scriptural twisting, contradict that? Let God be true and all others liars. The Bible clearly says that angels do not marry and that is what we ought to believe.

The fact is that even if those angels were to have come to earth, they were still angels and could not marry. They did not cease being angels just because they came to earth and took human form. They were still angels! Change of realm or position does not change the nature of beings from one into another. Humans or even angels do not change into something else when they go to different realms from theirs.

One other argument states that Jesus meant that only in heaven do angels not marry but that they could marry on earth. However, it is an argument based on a lack of proper understanding the true nature of the angels.

When Jesus said that angels in heaven do not marry, he was not talking of heaven *per se,* but implied the quality or nature of life there. He compared it to res-urrection life. He began his statement by saying, "For in the resurrection they neither marry, nor are given in marriage, but are as the angels of God in heaven" (Matthew 22:30).

The phrase, *"for in resurrection"* tells us that Jesus' subject was not heaven but resurrection. He was talking about resurrection life, which is other than the natural life known to man. Resurrection living is in the incor-ruptible realm of God in the spirit and is much more than life as known on earth. That is what Jesus was referring to, the *incorruptible* life.

This we can ascertain by reading this same discourse from the book of Luke.

> And Jesus answering said unto them, The
> children of this world marry, and are given in
> marriage: But they which shall be accounted
> worthy to obtain that world, and the resur-
> rection from the dead, neither *marry*, nor are
> given in marriage: Neither can they die any-
> more: for they are equal unto the angels; and
> are the children of God, being the children of
> the resurrection.
>
> Luke 20:34–36 (emphasis added)

This says that in this world people marry; whereas in that other world (realm), the realm of resurrection where angels are, there is no marriage. Hence, *it is not the angels' position of being in heaven what makes them not marry but rather the nature of their lives, as resurrection life.* Their nature does not allow them to marry whether in heaven or on earth. Thus, arguments that they could have married on earth is not true.

Angels Full of Lust

We have stated that resurrection life is totally contrary to and far superior to the natural one, even as heavens are far above the earth. It originates from perfect love what God is, and it has no lust in it. Lust is foreign to God's realm, as it is a part of the degenerating earthly life; it is a corruption in desire defined by the diction-ary *as bodily appetite, especially excessive sexual desire or an overmastering desire.* Thus, would it be possible that angels served in God's personal presence yet filled with excessive and overmastering sexual desires?

That would mean they were serving God; the God

of excellent glory within the incorruptible realm, yet somehow with their minds flirting out with women on earth! Is it possible that these angels dwelling under the power of God's divine nature were having such immoral thoughts? This further suggests that sexual lust found its way into the very presence of a holy, moral God brought there by his holy angels! Could this be the true God, who dwells in an unapproachable light that lights up everything and is himself a consuming fire?

If people understood God's *life*, they would not attribute such carnal thoughts to holy angels! It is difficult for such a scenario to be true. If this was to be, then the doctrine of God's immutability would have suffered irreparably if a change to the contrary could be found in him, especially condoning ungodliness in the so-called angel unholy flirting with women.

Another aspect of this whole thought to ponder is the fact that it must have taken some times for those angels to have come down to the human realm, arrange marriages, and then stay with their alleged wives until those wives gave birth to the said giants. That would not have been a short period of time! Could God with his eyes everywhere (according to Proverbs 15:3) have missed seeing those alleged angels sneaking down to women on earth? If he saw them was he powerless to stop them from such non-purposeful move in his plans?

All right, let's suppose that these fallen angels came down to earth and married the daughters of men as is taught in this doctrine. What does that tell us? It bespeaks that the Almighty God was outsmarted by his own creation, which sneaked out on him and disappeared to the earth to come wreak such acts of immorality upon mankind outside God's design and knowledge. Can this be true? How could it happen? Those angels allegedly sneaked out on God, who as to knowledge is omniscience and as to place is omnipresent, with non-slumbering eyes watching! Is that possible? And if it is, are we talking about the omnipotent, Almighty God?

The inference is that those fallen angels pulled a quick one on the Almighty God, who was then hard pressed to do something to save himself further embarrassment. Such reasoning portrays that that was the reason God brought the flood upon the earth. However, that is not true. The God who knows even when one sparrow falls to the ground and knows the very number of the hair on our head—do you think he could have missed out on those angels claimed to have come to earth from his personal presence? Is that possible?

Furthermore, the Bible says our God is able to keep especially his saints in this corrupt world.

> Now unto him that is able to keep you from falling, and to present you faultless before the presence of his glory with exceeding joy.
>
> Jude 1:24

God can keep his saints in this corrupt world and present them faultless unto him, yet he could not keep his angels in the celestial realm from lust! Nothing can be further from the truth.

Furthermore, Jesus' statement that in resurrection people will not marry does not even mean they will cease to be people.

> And Jesus answering said unto them, *The children of this world marry*, and are given in marriage: But *they which shall be accounted worthy to obtain that world*, and the resurrection from the dead, *neither marry, nor are given in marriage:* Neither can they die anymore: for they are equal unto the angels; and are the children of God, *being the children of the resurrection.*
>
> Luke 20:34–36 (emphasis added)

The children of this world marry, but children of the resurrection neither marry nor are given in marriage. They will still be people, men and women, but they will not marry. Why? Because they will be in a different plane or state of life where there will be no sexual urges. This is so because sex will be of no purpose then. It was given for the purpose of procreation and husband-wife enjoyment on the earth plane. But there will be no more of the enjoyment we derive from each other or other persons then, for our enjoyment will be the Lord God himself. Our main goal then will be God's exaltation and not the gratification of our personal appetites!

Every self-serving or desiring appetite will have been reoriented to point God-ward. And God himself will be the fulfillment of all our needs and desires. He alone will become the source of our joy. Sex as a function of human systems would have served its purpose on earth and ceased; Paul says that at the twinkling of an eye we shall be changed. Our faculties of flesh life will be changed and lifted to function on a higher plane within God's purposes. It means we will have been reconstituted to fit and function in that higher plane of living.

Creature Functioning outside God's Design

The creature cannot function outside its designed purpose. Is it possible for a creature to originate for itself something or a function God never intended for it? Is it possible for your knees to decide to begin seeing when they were not designed for that?

Moreover, in matters of sexology the experts say that humans' greatest sexual organ is their brain. This implies that no one can engage in sexual acts without brains. Every sexual act begins somewhere in the brain. Does this mean then those angels alleged to have engaged in sex with humans had brains? Remember brain is matter, whereas angels are non material spirit beings. Did these non-material beings posses a material part? If not, then how were their sexual experiences registered and programmed without the brain?

Furthermore, science (molecular biology) has so far found out that a woman's chromosomes will react differently to and even fail to aid the fertilization of sperms from a species of being that has a DNA other than human. What does this tell us of the possibility of these angels in impregnating the women? Without a change in their DNA to match that of the humans, it is questionable if they could impregnate the women.

God had instituted a creative law, which stipulated that "*every seed* thereof, *after its kind.*"

And God said, Let the earth bring forth grass, the herb yielding seed, and the fruit tree yielding fruit after his kind, whose seed is in itself, upon the earth: and it was so. And the earth brought forth grass, and herb yielding seed after his kind, and the tree yielding fruit, whose seed was in itself, after his kind: and God saw that it was good.

Genesis 1:11–12

He pronounced the law good and has not revoked it; humans still only bear humans and so forth. Every species can only produce within its category.

However, proponents of angel marriage imply that those angels were able to go against all those created in-built hurdles within nature to impregnate the women. That calls for a greater faith to believe it than just the simplicity of God's Word. It is man's word (interpretation) put alongside God's.

The Phrase *Sons of God*

We observed earlier that the reference *sons of God* is a *generic* term, which in its widest sense means more than just *male offspring*. But the sense in which it is employed in the angel-marriage teaching makes it mean male offspring only.

However, the *International Jewish Encyclopedia* says that the Hebrew phrase *Benei Elohim*, translated "sons of God," is used to describe angels with particular references to Job 1:6 and 38:7. But it is a *Hebrew idiom* which conveys the connectedness to God's holiness and power or separation and designation for God's holy purposes and according to Tanakh, it does not connote physical descent from or unity of essence with God.

It applies to a group or individuals uniquely set apart for God's divine purposes, a group that can be angels or human beings. It was also used to describe immensely authoritative people like judges or rulers or those endowed with godly graces. Hence, it necessarily does not and should not be restricted to mean angels only.

Also to be noted is the fact that, as a Hebraic idiom it does not mean what it seems to say for idiomatic expressions do not always mean the exact words that form them.

Hence, to restrict it or make it mean angels became *men* is to misapply its usage. The Bible calls Adam the son of God, which was the son of Enos, which was the son of Seth, which was the son of *Adam, which was the son of God* (Luke 3:38). Should we then not assume that Adam was himself an angel since the Bible calls him a son of God! You can see how doing that would be totally out of context. Besides, if angels were turning into humans, how come they all chose to turn only into men? Yet, the Bible says that *when men began to multiply on the face of the earth,* there was already tremendous increase in the number of men?

Furthermore, in the prophets, God in several places calls the Israelites his sons, should we then presume that they were angels? They were his sons though he did not bear them physically.

Fear not: for I am with thee: I will bring thy seed from the east, and gather thee from the west; I will say to the north, Give up; and to the south, Keep not back: bring my sons from far, and my daughters from the ends of the earth.

Isaiah 43:5–6

Yet the number of the children of Israel shall be as the sand of the sea, which cannot be measured nor numbered; and it shall come to pass, that in the place where it was said unto them, Ye are not my people, there it shall be said unto them, Ye are the sons of the living God.

Hosea 1:10

God personally promises to be a father to any people separated unto him:

Wherefore come out from among them, and be ye separate, saith the Lord, and touch not the unclean thing; and I will receive you. And will be a *Father unto you*, and ye shall be my sons and daughters.

2 Corinthians 6:17 -18(emphasis added)

Major Scriptures in Support of this View

Some of the backbone scriptures for this theory are Genesis 6:1–6, 2 Peter 2:4–6, and Jude 6–7.

Scripture Number One
Let us begin by looking at the Genesis account.

> And it came to pass, when men began to mul-
> tiply on the face of the earth, and daughters
> were born unto them, That the sons of God
> saw the daughters of men that they were fair;
> and they took them wives of all which they
> chose. And the LORD said, My spirit shall
> not always strive with man, for that he also
> is flesh: yet his days shall be a hundred and
> twenty years.
>
> There were giants in the earth in those
> days; and also after that, when the sons of
> God came in unto the daughters of men,
> and they bore children to them, the same
> became mighty men which were of old, men
> of renown.
>
> And GOD saw that the wickedness of
> man was great in the earth, and that every
> imagination of the thoughts of his heart was
> only evil continually.
>
> Genesis 6:1–5

From these verses, the angel-marriage proponents
make the phrase *sons of God* to mean angels, because it
is also used in Job 1:6, 2:1, 38:7 to refer to angels. It is true
angels were called sons of God, and we have explained
the reasons for that. Yet to assume that the same phrase
sons of God here means the same thing is to be out of
context. If we read it within context, especially without

introducing any thoughts as to it meaning angels, then we will easily get our bearing.

As a matter of fact, we have pointed out that so far from Genesis 1 up to this point there had been no mention of angels anywhere apart from the mention of Cherubim in Eden. The story so far has been about man, his glorious creation, unfortunate fall, and then the effects of that fall on his relationship with fellow man and God.

Genesis 1 introduces us to man, his creation, and God's intended purpose. Chapter two shows us man enjoying the garden and God's creation. Chapter three brings us to the unfortunate fall of man and his exiting Eden, the garden of the tree of life. Chapter four gives us a closer and detailed look at man after the fall living his life independent of God. Some preliminary effects of the fall are displayed in that chapter; especially after Cain killed his brother Abel. With that act, the spotlight is on Cain and those of his lineage in the rest of that chapter.

Chapter five then brings a contrast to Cain's life by introducing Seth and his lineage. That contrast shows a clear distinction between those two main camps then, though some schools of thought teach there was no difference. But if there was no specific distinction, why would God go into great details of showing us how Seth came from Adam up to the point in which his camp began to worship God? Chapter five ends with the mention of Noah, whom we later meet in chapter six. Is that just a coincidence?

Chapter six then brings us to man in a breakdown,

the breakdown of all demarcations of godlessness and godliness. There was a breakdown on the clear distinction of the two representative people groups, which resulted into corruption of character, and it affected life in general on earth. Man lived a mixture, neither this nor that. Clearly, the story so far has been all about man coming all the way from Adam.

Adam was called the son of God, and Seth whom we were introduced to in Genesis 4 in contrast to Cain carried over that lineage of *sonship*. But like the existence of God, this was not explicitly stated. Nonetheless, Adam called the son of God, had his offspring, Seth, named with him in the genealogy of Jesus. Cain, though first born, is not named in that genealogy; he had sealed his own fate by walking away from the Lord, rejecting all the mercies and grace, and became *a mere man*. This left Seth alone as the representative of the godly line on earth.

As such, the most acceptable interpretation and best view on the meaning of the phrase *sons of God* in the Genesis account is that which refers to the lineage of Seth, whom God gave Adam and Eve as a replacement after Cain killed Abel.

For that reason, his lineage by implication was the *sons of God* that became the representative of godliness then. It does not mean everyone in it was perfect but that was the representative godly lineage in comparison to Cain's, which was considered completely ungodly.

God's way of determining righteousness or godliness is quite different from humans.' Remember Lot, Abraham's nephew; the self-centered, self-serving fellow who moved to Sodom and integrated well into the culture of that city's life to the point he was ready to give over his daughters for immoral sexual indulgences. What a great compromiser we can say! Yet, the Bible calls him righteous Lot (2 Peter 2:7–8), and God rescued him from Sodom!

In the Old Testament, God imputed (not imparted) righteousness to people based on their faith in him. For example, righteousness was credited to Abraham because of his faith in God, not that he was perfect! And Lot, who the Bible calls righteous, must also have received it only by God's credit, God having observed faith in his heart in spite of himself!

However, by saying this I am not justifying contrary living; I am only trying to underscore the fact that God determines who his real people are by their hearts, in relations to his purposes. He is not looking for perfect people but those he can perfect himself.

Hence, it is shear indifference for anyone to insinuate that there was no difference between *Seth's lineage* and Cain's. The *Sethites* who had been separated unto God's divine purposes were the ones referred to as sons of God. They believed in God to the level that they began to worship him. The Bible clearly says that it was in Seth's time that people began to call on the Lord (Genesis 4:26). With such practical faith in their hearts, what makes anyone think God could not or did not credit righteousness to them? In fact, later on we meet Noah, a *Sethite* called a righteous man: righteous but not perfect!

It is this Noah who met the demands of a holy God

in his generation. His lifestyle displayed his heart condition and made God appoint him to the building of the Ark. In the midst of the breakdown, God found a man to work with, someone who obeyed him without questioning. He was from Seth's godly representative lineage.

How the Distinctions Came About

After killing his brother Abel, Cain refused to repent when God confronted him with his sin. Instead he hardened his heart and likely got into an argument with God over his sinful act. He claimed he was not responsible for his brother's welfare. God then cursed the ground on which he had put his trust as his source of livelihood. He then went away from the Lord's presence.

> And Cain went out from the presence of the LORD, and dwelt in the land of Nod, on the east of Eden.
>
> Genesis 4:16

Away from God, he became his own person, totally divorced from God, living all for himself. Thus, without God he then became a mere man, and his descendants became sons and daughters of *man*.

However, though mere men, they were a people of great talents and abilities. Genesis 4 gives the details of their exploits. It was within Cain's descendants that we find pastoralists and businessmen. There were also great musicians in that lineage, handling harp and organs. In fact, Jubal, one of Cain's great, great grandsons was the inventor of those musical instruments. His name Jubal means music.

Hence, in this camp we find businessmen, herds-men, and musicians. Together with that there were also jewelers and smiths dealing in brass and iron. They were the high-tech people then. There are also implica-tions that there were beauticians and models too from this lineage.

Lamech, one of Cain's great grandsons, had mar-ried two wives: Adah and Zillah respectively. The name Adah means beauty or ornament. Hence, here we see beauty in this camp. But it was not beauty alone; that same man Lamech had a daughter called Naamah, a name that means sweet or pleasant. As such, in the circle of children of men, their daughters were not only beautiful but pleasant too. They seemed good to hang out with, for they were known for their beauty and pleasantness.

Thus, when the Bible says, "And it came to pass, when men began to multiply on the face of the earth, *and daughters were born unto them,* That the sons of God saw *the daughters of men* that they were *fair,*" it is talking about those beautiful and pleasant women from Cain's lineage (Genesis 6:1–2, emphasis added). They were fair, beautiful, and pleasant. The reference "daughters of men" could not have meant women in general, as then there was a clear distinction between people living for God referred to as sons of God and those living for themselves, as mere men. It is sheer denial for anyone to claim there were no clear differences.

Those who did not care the least about sin and evil

were from Cain's lineage, where up to then there had been two murders recorded (Genesis 4:23). Those who loved God were from Seth's lineage; in fact the Bible says it was during Seth's time that people began to worship God (Genesis 4:26). While the others were living for themselves, murdering each other and involving in various selfish acts, this other group was worshipping the God of heaven.

These worshippers from Seth's line were called sons of God because they had chosen to love and worship him. This does not mean they were perfect in their relationship with him; however, they loved and trusted him and accordingly they represented his interest in the earth then. They were considered his sons. They were believers, and all who believed and accepted God he gave power to become his sons. That was a principle then and even later in the New Testament.

> But as many as received him, to them gave he power to become the sons of God, even to them that believe on his name.
>
> John 1:12

Nevertheless, as population from both sides increased, it reached a time when the men from Seth's lineage got tired of the monotony of just relating to women from their own camp. Seemingly, those women were familiar to them, and as has been said, familiarity breeds contempt. They were contemptuous of and did not like their own women anymore. They likely needed a new thing, new relationships that would thrill them!

They wanted the freedom to get women described as fair (pleasant and beautiful) from the other camp.

Thereby, slowly by slowly they begun and finally broke loose from their convictions about God and the related matters. They left the restraints of the godly lifestyles to follow the dictates of their own feelings. They lost sight of their purpose as the chosen people; then intrigue and rebellion plagued their lives. They plunged headlong into the world of meaninglessness, drifting about in life with their sole interest being fulfilling the lusts of their flesh. In the book of Proverbs the Bible says:

> In the house of the [uncompromisingly] righteous is great [priceless] treasure, but with the income of wicked is trouble and vexation.
>
> Proverbs 15:6 (AMP)

As long as these Sethites were non-compromising, they stood as great and priceless treasures of God in the earth. But when they left their stand for God, trouble and vexation set in. They saw the daughters of men (Cainites) to be fair and then made random choices of women from them. And that is what the record talks about, that the sons of God (the Sethites) saw the daughters of men (the Cainites) that they were fair and they took them wives of all which they chose. *This has nothing to do with angels.* It is humans, who can marry other humans. If angels were to marry at all, they could only marry angels as their natures are compatible!

Scripture Number Two

The angel-marriage teaching also appeals to 2 Peter 2:4–6 to justify its claim that *sons of God* means angels. Let us look at it:

> For if God spared not the angels that sinned, but cast them down to hell, and delivered them into chains of darkness, to be reserved unto judgment;
>
> And spared not the old world, but saved Noah the eighth person, a preacher of righteousness, bringing in the flood upon the world of the ungodly;
>
> And turning the cities of Sodom and Gomorrah into ashes condemned them with an overthrow, making them an example unto those that after should live ungodly.
>
> 2 Peter 2:4–6

The interpretation here is alleged that these scriptures connect the angels that sinned with the world of Noah's day and the evil cities of Sodom and Gomorrah. It is purported that those verses read something like, "For if God spared not the angels that sinned ... And spared not the old world, but saved Noah ... And turning the cities of Sodom and Gomorrah into ashes."

Since there is the mentioning of Noah and the cities of Sodom and Gomorrah immediately after talking about the fallen angels, this is said to create a connection between these different times. It is made to appear as though the fallen angels came down during Noah's time and corrupted the women. And that they later came down into Sodom and Gomorrah, causing the unprecedented immorality. But this is totally untrue. It misses the concepts of what Peter is trying to communicate here; such an interpretation is out of context of Peter's message.

If properly understood, Peter is listing the major catastrophic judgments God had meted on rebellion to his rule of righteousness. He begins with the very first one ever, the judgment meted upon the rebellious angels. There had never been any judgment to be cited, so Peter had to begin with the very first one ever meted. Then he moves on to the next serious judgment, which occurred in the human history during Noah's time. Between the angelic rebellion and the judgment of Noah's day, there was no major judgment to mention, though some folks talk of Cain's judgment. But that was not in the category of catastrophic judgments and as such, Peter found it insignificant to mention.

Accordingly, we find that the angelic judgment was followed by the Noah's day judgment. This did not mean there was a connection between those fallen angels and Noah's day. It was not those rebel angels who came down on earth and directly got involved with women bringing corruption and God's wrath! Such an interpretation is totally out of context and would raise more questions than answers!

Even if this was to be true that those angels came to earth, they could only have found a fertile ground for such alleged activities between them and women already existing in man. Man was already in worse moral conditions, even without those alleged angels. Man had sold out to sin and was already in a terrible condition of wickedness. Verse three of Genesis 6 depicts that God's Spirit had been in constant striving with man, convicting and convincing him of the need to live by God's precepts.

But man in selfishness and rebellion continued doing his own things. He did not care the least about God. As a result, God announced he was not going to keep on chasing after man in his willful rebellion. He was ready to withdraw his Spirit from striving with man. His entire concern up to that point was man; there is not even an insinuation anywhere that any of the angels (sons of God) was responsible for man's condition then.

Genesis 6:5 goes on to talk about man's condition, with God then pinpointing man's exact areas of problems and its results. God indicated that man's source of problems was his *heart and thoughts were evil*. God did not attribute man's deplorable condition to some angels or anything, but the wicked heart of man. Man was contaminated by sin within his nature. This resulted in great wickedness in the earth. The earth was already corrupted by man's wickedness.

Thus, it is illogical to claim that only when angels alleged to have turned into men came that is when immorality became rampant on earth. Sexual immorality and violence were already on earth then. It all sprang up from the human sinful heart, and God was ready to judge it even without any slight inference to angelic involvement.

As such, if there were to be any angels that could have been attracted to and by such situations, they too must have been wicked and could not have been referred to as the sons of God! Yet, the angels here alleged to have come and married the daughters of men were called "sons of God." This implies they could not have been the fallen angels! This reference was only used of angels when they were on God's side. The fallen angels did not retain that depiction after they fell; further more that reference "sons of God" associated such angels more with God than Satan.

> Now there was a day when the sons of God came to present themselves before the LORD, and Satan came also among them.
>
> Job 1:6

From this scripture, the understanding is that Satan was not included in the reference "the sons of God." It says that the sons of God came and Satan came also. Satan was not at that point of existence counted one with the sons of God. Therefore, these angels called the sons of God must have been those directly from his presence. But just how could a whole lot of angels from God's presence take to such wickedness! Did anything about God change then?

Nevertheless, Genesis 6 states that man continued in his willful rebellion against God, and finally God pronounced his judgment. But notice that God's judgment was a judgment on man not on angels. Up till that time there had been no mention of or even mere inference to angels! The story so far has been focused on human beings. It was not the alleged angels' involvement with women that brought God's wrath, but man's wickedness. And that wickedness was not only sexual immorality as the emphasis seems to be from the proponents of this teaching; it included violence and all other kinds of human corruptions.

> The earth also was corrupt before God, and the earth was filled with violence. And God looked upon the earth, and, behold, it was corrupt; for all flesh had corrupted his way upon the earth.
>
> Genesis 6:11–12

God's judgment came to the earth not because of angels, but because of man's prideful hardened heart toward God. No one seemed to respond to God's Spirit's striving with man, except Noah, who then found grace before God.

Thus, these are some of the points Peter was trying to bring out. So from the judgment of Noah's day, Peter then moves to the next major catastrophic judgment, meted upon the cities of Sodom and Gomorrah. This is the business Peter is involved with here; listing all those major judgments, which in fact marked God's new phase of involvement with his people.

Peter did that sending out a warning based on the precedence of what God had done. He was, in other words, warning that if God had done it before, he is able and can do it again. He was warning that God would bring judgment upon all those twisting his word to mislead people from him. Peter was not saying that those rebel angels came down during Noah's time, messed up sexually with the women, and the situation became like Sodom and Gomorrah! If it were to be interpreted like that, then it would even raise more question than it answers. Questions like, does it mean then that the angels who fell only did it as recently as during Noah's time, yet scriptural inferences seem to indicate that the rebellion occurred long before the creation of man and even the earth? Or does this mean there have been two angelic rebellions so far?

The best way to catch what Peter is really saying here is to read those portions of scriptures independently without the input of these people's interpretations.

Scripture Number Three

Let us also look at Jude 5–7, which the proponents of the angel-marriage theory appeal to too:

> I will therefore put you in remembrance, though ye once knew this, how that the Lord, having saved the people out of the land of Egypt, afterward destroyed them that believed not.
>
> And the angels which kept not their first estate, but left their own habitation, he hath reserved in everlasting chains under darkness unto the judgment of the great day.
>
> Even as Sodom and Gomorrah, and the cities about them in like manner, giving themselves over to fornication, and going after

strange flesh, are set forth for an example, suffering the vengeance of eternal fire.

Jude 1:5–7

Angel-marriage teachers claim these verses also
carry similar sentiments to those of 2 Peter we have
looked at above. From these verses in Jude, they deduce
that these angels (a) left their own estate, (b) gave
themselves over to fornication, (c) went after strange
flesh! But wait a minute, look at those verses carefully.
Who gave themselves to fornication and went after
strange flesh? It was not the angels but the Sodomites
and the cities about them, which is what verse seven
says. Claiming it was the angels who did this is making
the Bible say what it does not; that is reading into the
Bible what one already has in his or her mind!

However, Jude, like Peter, is listing and warning
about the past judgments of God. He begins with the
Hebrews history well known to those he was writing to
then. But Jude goes a little further than Peter; he adds
something to his information. He names the judgments and the reasons for them. According to him, the
Hebrews were delivered but due to continued unbelief
were judged with destruction.

From the well-known Hebrews' history, Jude then
continues his listing by going back to the very first
major judgment God ever meted: the judgment upon
the rebel angels. Jude says that these angels' sin was that
they left their first estate. These fallen angels left their
own rightful estate or habitation; however, that they
did just within their realm. They did not change worlds

to cross over into the human plane like the angel-marriage teaching would have us believe. The power to change themselves into something else and hence escape the celestial realm was not inherent in them. As such, if they left their rightful abode, that definitely was still within the celestial realm. But exactly where they went we have not been told.

Thus, instead of speculating that they must have come to earth, we should understand that the earth was not the only place within the created existence. But the angel-marriage teachers seem to think that there are only two spheres, earth and heaven. Hence, they reason that when such angels left their abode (thought to have been in heaven) then they must have come to earth. But that is an erroneous and limited thinking.

I suggest that those angels teamed up with Lucifer and tried to rise above the exalted throne of God, only to eventually find that finally they lost even their usual celestial abode. They left their estate trying to ascend to and go beyond God's throne. But then they were arrested and committed in chains to dark dungeons of hell awaiting their doom. This must have been long, long before even the creation of the humans. Their punishment was they were now reserved in chains.

Jude then moves on to the examples of the cities of Sodom and Gomorrah, telling us of their sin: they gave themselves over to fornication and went after strange flesh. He then mentions their punishment as, *suffering the vengeance of eternal fire.*

For clarity purposes, we can portray what Jude is saying as follows:

Table 1

The Judgment Meted on	Reasons for It	Punishment for It
1. Israelites	Persistent unbelief	Destruction
2. Fallen angels	Left their estate	Chained in darkness
3. Sodom and Gomorrah	Perverse sexual immorality	Overthrown by fire

Jude, like Peter, was warning that since God in the past had judged seriously without respect to persons, he would do it again if need be, especially against those who persist in sin, which in Jude 4 he refers to as those turning God's grace into a license to sin!

The very reason for writing his letter is well covered in verses one through three. His main concern was that the brethren, who had been called of God sanctified by him and preserved in Christ, were to earnestly contend for the faith, which was once delivered unto the saints. They were to preserve it even if through perseverance and only through God's ever new mercies, peace, and love. That means they were to defend it vigorously and by all means within Christian principles based on love.

He then goes on to explain the consequences of not guarding and keeping that which God entrusts to a people. In fact, that is where his warning springs from. All these warnings, beginning with the Israelites, the fallen angels, and Sodom and Gomorrah, were being listed as a warning to those who do not keep earnestly that which God entrusts to them. This was especially to those who had turned God's grace into a license for sin. They wanted to continue in sin and enjoy grace at the same time, disregarding Paul's clear teaching on the same.

> What shall we say, then? Should we continue to live in sin so that God's grace will increase? Certainly not! We have died to sin—how then can we go on living in it?
>
> Romans 6:1–2 (GNB)

Those who read the Book of Jude and misconstrue, he was building the "fallen angels connection to Noah's day and Sodom and Gomorrah" are necessarily wrong. It is ridiculous, unscriptural, and wrong for them to turn these statements around to refer to the fallen angels. The fallen angels were not the subject of Jude's address, especially in verse seven. The subject of verse seven was Sodom and Gomorrah. We can verify this by simply reading Jude from verse five and skipping verse six and jumping to seven. Let's see how.

> I will therefore put you in remembrance, though ye once knew this, how that the Lord, having saved the people out of the land of Egypt, afterward destroyed them that believed not.
>
> Jude 1:5

> Even as Sodom and Gomorrah, and the cities about them in like manner, giving themselves over to fornication, and going after strange flesh, are set forth for an example, suffering the vengeance of eternal fire.
>
> Jude 1:7

If we read verses five and seven, can we then infer that it was the Israelites who gave themselves over to fornication and went after strange flesh? Everyone can clearly see that that is not the case. But then why would that be the case when verse six is read and followed by seven, yet each of these verses is a complete example in itself?

All right, even if we can turn verse seven to talk about those fallen angels, how did they give themselves to fornication then? It is purported they came to earth and *married* the daughters of men. Is marriage fornication? Fornication is an illegitimate sexual act involving unmarried persons, yet it is purported these angels were married. The biblical record does not read that those angels gave themselves over to adultery, but reads that Sodom and Gomorrah, and the cities about them, gave themselves over to fornication, and going after strange flesh. This portion of the scriptures is clearly not referring to the fallen angels but the sodomites.

How about the *strange flesh* part? Where is it in Genesis 6 account? How could they (angels) give themselves to strange flesh when they were never flesh in the first place? The book of Romans by inference speaks about strange flesh in the following terms, *those who dishonor their own bodies between themselves*, or *change the natural use for the unnatural*. This has the meaning of the same-sex relations. Is this what the angels did, *dishonoring their own bodies between themselves*? Did they then need to come down for the women if they could *dishonor their own bodies between themselves*? Yet, for this to be true, it would have required angels of flesh, and there are no angels of flesh!

In some modified form of the same teaching, there are those who to account for the flesh factor in angels claim that those angels came but did not marry the women directly. It is claimed those angels possessed men as their agents of expression, who then cohabited with the daughters of men. But that too is an insinuation that does not add up. Angels do not possess people.

Thus, generally speaking, the interpretation that angels came and married humans is just totally wrong. It is false scripturally as we have tried to point out; scientifically it is impossible. Naturally and logically it does not add up; while intellectually it is mind boggling! It is devoid of spirituality, only built on human carnality trying to shift blame for man's sin problem to angels. It is wrong from its very foundational suppositions, which are basically false assumptions!

5. *Do angels have meals, for the Bible in the book of Psalm 78:25 states that man did eat angels' food? If not what does that verse mean?*

Answer: To answer this question we need to read that Scripture from the previous verse, 24:

> And had rained down manna upon them to eat, and had given them of the corn of heaven. Man did eat angels' food: he sent them meat to the full.
>
> Psalm 78:24–25

It has long been presumed that the angels' food spoken of here was manna. Someone said that that sense of speech was just a metaphor depicting manna as such an important heavenly food (so delicate and so free from the ordinary coarse properties of food that it might be supposed to be such as angels feed on), but not necessarily that angels eat.

Targum, (the Aramaic translation of the Hebrew Bible) brings it out that *the children of men did eat food, which came down from the habitation of angels.* This seems to say they ate food prepared in the realm of the angels or prepared by angels; hence, the term angels' food. It is not food angels eat but rather prepared or watched prepared and served from their realm by them.

However, if it is the food angels eat, we are not clearly told so. We are not sure that in the celestial realm angels eat or even if they do where they get their food and so forth. But mention is made of "angels' food," and this somehow has been taken by others to mean that angels might be eating in their realm, though in their own way. Since they have a perpetual life; it would mean that their eating is not for their survival. In other words, they do not eat to live. Their eating could mainly be a kind of fun thing they are allowed to enjoy. Because life in that realm is regenerative, things like waste are nonexistent. Thus, food eaten would all seem to get absorbed into one's system with no waste to expect. Furthermore, the nature of their food seems to be superior to ours; it also must be spiritual food.

The Bible records that Prophet Elijah ate the angel food and walked over two hundred miles over a period of more than one and half months without getting tired or hungry again! This was after he took two angelic meals and a drink. He never thirsted, yet he trekked in the dry, hot, and sunny Damascus wilderness.

> And as he lay and slept under a juniper tree, behold, then an angel touched him, and said unto him, Arise and eat. And he looked, and,

behold, there was a cake baked on the coals, and a cruse of water at his head. And he did eat and drink, and laid him down again.

And the angel of the LORD came again the second time, and touched him, and said, Arise and eat; because the journey is too great for thee. And he arose, and did eat and drink, and went in the strength of that meat forty days and forty nights unto Horeb the mount of God."

Kings 19:5–8

Yet, among the angelic appearances down here on earth, there are clear records that they have eaten human food. Refer to Genesis 18:3–8.

6. *What can you say about the elect angels, who are they?*

Answer: In the realms of created intelligent beings, those referred to as the elect, implies there are those deemed as the rejected. The elect are those who have willfully chosen or elected to accept God's authority over them, while the rejects are those who have rejected God and will eventually be rejected themselves, in the end. Within the human realm, this is seen where some people reject God and his offer of life through his Son, while others accept him.

And then will I profess unto them, I never knew you: depart from me, ye that work iniquity. Then shall he say also unto them on the left hand, Depart from me, ye cursed, into everlasting fire, prepared for the devil and his angels.

Matthew 7:23, 25:41

This is speaking of those who will be rejected by the Lord in the end. They will find themselves in company of the devil and his angels in their condemned destination. But generally speaking, the elect angels are those who remained faithful to God when Satan led a rebellion against him.

7. *You mentioned that some angels have wings. Are they feather wings or what type?*

Answer: This question seems more motivated by curiosity than with the desire of a true searching heart. But anyway, the Bible does not specifically say whether these angels have feathered wings or not. It only mentions they have wings. They may be feather wings or not. I am not sure. I think when wings are mentioned most people immediately only visualize birds. But it is not true that to have wings one must have feathers! Birds have feathers on their wings because that is what is all over their bodies; it is part of their nature. I, therefore, tend to think that these angelic wings must have been made from the same stuff their spiritual bodies are made from. The main point here is you do not need feathers to have wings; airplanes have wings but no feathers! Consider even creatures like moths and butterflies; they have wings that are in accord to the nature of their bodies, not feather wings. Even bats have wings but not feather wings!

Other contributing factors to angelic feather-wings notion are the many artistic depictions of angels either as babies or grown ups having wings or something. But these are not the reality; they are just the artists' impressions of what they imagined the angels would look like. People's own imaginations should not be used as the measure of truth.

8. *In the human world, when people fight, they kill each other. What happens in the angelic realm where they cannot die?*

Answer: The first point to make clear here is the fact that angels do not fight or war amongst themselves. Their conflict involves those rebel angels, who are against God and his plans. They try to hinder, slow, thwart, delay, and destroy God's plans. But then that is where the point of the conflict arises. However, this conflict is not meant to finish or kill the enemy at this time; that has been reserved for a later time. The conflict now is mainly to restrain, defeat, deter, and chase away the enemy from hindering or distracting God's good plans for his creation. The angels involved in this warfare are only enforcers of God's commands to make sure everything goes on as God has decreed or planed. They are not to kill or finish the enemy, not even to rail against them.

Yet Michael the archangel, when contending with the devil he disputed about the body of

Moses, durst not bring against him a railing accusation, but said, The Lord rebuke thee.

Jude 1:9

Therefore, there is no killing in the sense that we know of or any of such things in the angelic warfare. Angels only fight to dispel, defeat, chase away the enemy, and establish God's order and authority for the fulfillment of his purposes until his appointed time.

9. *What do angels exactly look like?*

Answer: We do not exactly know what angels look like; we have not been clearly told. But in terms of explaining what they seem to look like, we will have to look from both their and our realms. Whenever angels appear on earth to various individuals, they normally assume human form dependent on their specific mission at that time. This seems to suggest they are not in human form in their realm and how they appear to us here is not what they are in their place. What they exactly look like in their realm is something else. This assertion concurs with the descriptions of both cherubim and seraphim as found in the Bible.

The Bible in Ezekiel describes the cherubim as four-faced, four-winged beings. Their celestial appearance is breathtaking and their description awesome.

> Also out of the midst thereof came the like-
> ness of four living creatures. And this was
> their appearance; they had the likeness of a

man. And every one had four faces, and every one had four wings.

And their feet were straight feet; and the sole of their feet was like the sole of a calf's foot: and they sparkled like the color of burnished brass. And they had the hands of a man under their wings on their four sides; and they four had their faces and their wings.

Their wings were joined one to another; they turned not when they went; they went every one straight forward. As for the likeness of their faces, they four had the face of a man, and the face of a lion, on the right side: and they four had the face of an ox on the left side; they four also had the face of an eagle.

Thus were their faces: and their wings were stretched upward; two wings of every one were joined one to another, and two covered their bodies. And they went every one straight forward: whither the spirit was to go, they went; and they turned not when they went.

Ezekiel 1:5–12

Oh, what awesome beings these cherubim are! Their description continues in that whole chapter. Ezekiel's description befits the cherubim because they are *four winged*. From this we learn that angels as they are in God's presence are quite different from what man is allowed to see when they appear here.

Let's move over to the book of Revelation for the descriptions of the seraphim by the Apostle John.

And immediately I was in the spirit: and, behold, a throne was set in heaven, and one sat on the throne. And he that sat was to look upon like a jasper and a sardine stone: and there was a rainbow round about the throne, in sight like unto an emerald.

And round about the throne were four and twenty seats: and upon the seats I saw four and twenty elders sitting, clothed in white raiment; and they had on their heads crowns of gold. And out of the throne proceeded lightnings and thunderings and voices: and there were seven lamps of fire burning before the throne, which are the seven Spirits of God.

And before the throne there was a sea of glass like unto crystal: and in the midst of the throne, and round about the throne, were four beasts full of eyes before and behind. And the first beast was like a lion, and the second beast like a calf, and the third beast had a face as a man, and the fourth beast was like a flying eagle.

And the four beasts had each of them six wings about him; and they were full of eyes within: and they rest not day and night, saying, Holy, holy, holy, Lord God Almighty, which was, and is, and is to come.

Revelation 4:4–8

This description fits the seraphim, because they are *six winged* according to the Prophet Isaiah.

> Above it [God's throne] stood the Seraphims: each one had six wings with twain he covered his face, and with twain he covered his feet, and with twain he did fly. And one cried unto another, and said, Holy, holy, holy, is the LORD of hosts: the whole earth is full of his glory.
>
> Isaiah 6:2–3

Their position is mentioned to be in the midst of and round about the throne. From scriptures, cherubim are on either side of the throne. In fact, the Bible says God dwells between the cherubim. But it is the seraphim who are directly associated with the throne, converging around and directly above it and in the center or midst of it.

John's description continues that these beings were saying holy, holy, holy Lord God Almighty who was and is and is to come. This is what the seraphim are known for, proclaiming God's holiness. But from John's description it is as though he was only having a single dimensional view and only saw four of these beings. There could have been more, but John was only able to see four. The WILLIAMS New Testament and the AMPlified Bible in Revelation 4:6 lead to the conclusion they may have been more than just the four.

WILLIAMS New Testament reads:

> Also in front of the throne there was something like a sea of glass as clear as crystal. Around the throne, at the middle of each side

were four living creatures dotted with eyes in front and behind.

Revelation 4:6 (WILLIAMS)

The phrase "at the middle of each side were four living creatures," clearly suggests there must have been more than only four. At times in situations like those, people do not take many details, even the Prophet Isaiah did not state any numbers in regard to the seraphim he saw. It is, therefore, clear that John only looked from a certain vantage point, for he was only able to see one dimension of the four faced angels. John is more or less seeing similar beings to Ezekiel, except he was not able to get the full view of their four faces, as Ezekiel did. He only describes the single faces!

Therefore, the descriptions here show that these two groups of angels are almost the same, except for the number of their wings and their positions or stations in relation to God's throne. What John and Ezekiel are describing are not things they saw when angels appeared to them on earth but rather what they saw when ushered into the celestial realm. This to my understanding is what angels look like in their realm, though human minds cannot comprehend it easily and we cannot even say how they exactly look like!

God does not allow them to carry their celestial image into the earthly realm. He makes them only appear to us in acceptable ways, allowing them to assume a form that is conceivable and appropriate to us. Otherwise, no one would stand to receive a message from a four-face, four-winged being claiming to have come from God. Some of us would just fall dead at such a sight. I believe even our formed image of God is quite different from the reality of who he is in his realm. That means we will all be awestruck when we finally see God face to face.

10. *Some people teach that cherubim and seraphim are not angels but amongst the spirit beings in heaven. Do you subscribe to this view, and what is the truth about it?*

Answer: I think those who deny that cherubim and seraphim are angels do so still holding to the earlier century teachings, which did not conceive these two in the angelic hierarchy. They were thought not to be angels and as such were not grouped amongst the angels. There was a persistent confusion on this arising from the various theological positions taken by the church fathers like St. Ambrose, St. Jerome, and Thomas Aquinas, who were the authorities in such matters then. They never agreed on anything as touching angels. Each of them had his own conclusions, and so there existed that stand off, for no one wanted to be thought to support any of those positions. Later on, it was reported that Bishop Theodorus of Heracleâa, declared that seraphim and cherubim were not angels but rather averred they were horrible appearance of beasts meant to scare Adam from Eden.

Hence, by that pronouncement from the bishop, the angelic hierarchy could not list them as angels. As a matter of fact, the angelic hierarchy differed greatly depending on the source and the authority one consulted, but most of them listed seraphim in the highest order followed by cherubim. However, some listings omitted *seraphim*, *cherubim*, and *thrones*. Thus, the hierarchy listing ranged from between six to twelve levels depending on which authority you consulted. But the main and dominant hierarchy was thought to be nine levels, and this was held as the earlier Orthodox teachings on the holy angels by the Catholics and even Orthodox.

However, after theological development in later years when the Apostle Paul's usage of the terms *principalities*, *thrones*, *dominions* and *powers*, earlier taken to be part of the angelic hierarchy was understood; then seraphim and cherubim were permanently added into the angelic category.

Nonetheless, the reason some folks do not consider seraphim and cherubim as angels is also because they presume that angels should just look the same in their realm as they do when they appear on earth. Some of such people are naturalists to whom even the supernatural should look the same. But as explained in the question above, angels' appearances to humans on earth are not necessarily what they look like in God's presence! The descriptions of the cherubim or seraphim as seen in Ezekiel and Revelation is awesome and has no resemblance at all to any already formed images in our minds about angels. Their appearances before God is definitely different from what we know or thought we did. Therefore, judging by their appearances before God, such people draw conclusions that these beings must not be angels!

However, denying that cherubim are angels infers that Lucifer himself, who the Bible says was an "anointed cherub," was not an angel in the first place. This then raises more questions than answers. Who are those angels recorded to have fallen with him? They are called the devil and his angels (Matthew 25:41). If Lucifer was not an angel, then how comes he only found a following from among the angels? Why aren't there any "cherubic beings" amongst the host led by Satan? That would be like saying some man led a rebellion against some king, only to find a following from monkeys, with no human beings as part of his campaign. Would that be normal? It would be very odd indeed!

The Bible in general reference calls all of them the angels who kept not their first estate but left their own habitation (Jude 1:6). Lucifer is included in that, being called an angel. Even considering our first reference to the devil and his angels, the Bible uses the same expression when talking about Michael the archangel. Michael and his angels fought against the dragon, and the dragon fought and his angels (Revelation 12:7). The phrase *and his angels* is used here too. Does it mean Michael was a different being from the angels here called "his angels"? Of course not.

Why then would the devil be considered different from those called "his angels" in the phrase "the devil and his angels"? In fact, doing that makes Jesus, who made this reference, a liar, for he called or classified the devil with the fallen angels!

Nevertheless, it can be seen that making cherubim and seraphim different and separate beings from angels requires lots of scriptural reinterpretations to make sense. However, from scriptures it is clear that cherubim and seraphim are among the angelic beings.

11. *What about the Angel of the Lord? Is it true he was the pre-incarnate Christ, and how could he be an angel and God at the same time?*

Answer: It is generally agreed amongst biblical scholars who believe in the pre-existence of Christ that the Angel of the Lord in the Old Testament was his pre-incarnate appearance. Thorough biblical studies have led to that conclusion. They hold that the Angel of the Lord was a theophany or Christophany, having introduced himself to Moses in the burning bush as God.

> And the angel of the LORD appeared unto him in a flame of fire out of the midst of a bush: and he looked, and, behold, the bush burned with fire, and the bush was not consumed. Moreover he said, I am the God of thy father, the God of Abraham, the God of Isaac, and the God of Jacob. And Moses hid his face; for he was afraid to look upon God.
>
> Exodus 3:2, 6

Therefore, it emerges that this Angel of the Lord is God. Yet in Zechariah 1:12, we find him praying to another person also called God concerning the cities of Jerusalem and Judah. He was in fact interceding for those cities to receive mercy. But how could he pray to himself? Is there a contradiction here? No, he was not praying to himself, but as part and parcel of the Godhead he must have been interceding to the Father. Therefore, we see that the Angel of the Lord is God, yet somewhat distinct from God. His intercessory ministry is clearly brought out here, further denoting he was Christ. Since there is unparalleled similarity between the ministry of the Angel of the Lord and Christ's, the conclusion is that He was one and the same person.

Moreover, someone added that God often appeared to people in the Old Covenant as the Angel of the Lord (Judges 6:20; 2 Samuel. 24:16; 1 Kings 19:5–7). This Angel of the Lord appeared to Hagar and spoke as though he was God, and Hagar herself called him God (Genesis. 16:7–13). The Bible says that the Angel of the Lord appeared to Moses in a burning bush, but it then says God himself spoke to Moses out of that burning bush (Exodus 3; Acts 7:30–38). The Angel of the Lord also appeared to Israel in Judges 2:1–5 and spoke as God. Judges 6:11–24 describes the appearance of the Angel of the Lord to Gideon and then says the Lord looked on Gideon. The Angel of the Lord even appeared to Manoah and his wife (Samson's parents), and they believed they had seen God (Judges 13:2–23). This angel, therefore, was not just one among the innumerable messengers of God but a deity himself.

His deity can be seen from the fact that He:-

1. Is identified as God (Genesis 16:7–13; 18:2–3; 22:1–18; Exodus 3:2–28; Judges 2:1–5; 6:11–16).

2. Is recognized as God (Genesis 16:9–13; 18:2–13; 22:1–18; Exodus 3:2–28; Judges 2:1–5; 6:11–16).

3. Is described in terms befitting deity alone (Exodus 3:5–14; Joshua 5:15).

4. Calls himself God (Genesis 31:11–13; Exodus 3:2–14).

5. Receives worship (Joshua 5:14; Judges 2:4).

6. Speaks with divine authority (Judges 2:1–5)

However, he was referred to as an angel not in the sense that he was a created being, but as sent from the Father as a messenger of the Lord. That might have been his reason for mostly referring to God in the book of John as "the one who sent me." He was not an angel—the created spirit being—but one carrying the Father's message to the needy humanity. He was the sent one. He was at that point in time an envoy—an emissary, if you will—from the Father sent, but he was not in any way inferior.

12. *There is also the teaching that Michael the archangel is in fact Jesus. Is it true?*

Answer: This is a doctrine common with a number of Christian groups, mostly those with Adventist backgrounds and some so-called Bible students. But from the outset, it is not biblically true; *Jesus* is not Michael, though some earlier Christian writings carried some inferences to that effect. But such were not authentic.

Michael is only and always referred to within the angelic contexts, outside of which you never hear of him. The reason is because he is an angel, a created spirit being very distinct and different from Jesus the Christ. The Bible calls him "one of the chief princes," meaning there were other princes who Michael was ranked equal to or among. If he were Jesus, the Bible would have called him Michael the *chief prince* or some other title setting him apart from all the rest. But it did not; rather it grouped him together with others of those "chief princes." Yet Jesus Christ stands alone.

> For by him were all things created, that are in heaven, and that are in earth, visible and invisible, whether they be thrones, or dominions, or principalities, or powers: all things were created by him, and for him: And he is before all things, and by him all things consist.
>
> Colossians 1:16–17

Let's read this from Williams New Testament.

> For it was through him that everything was created in heaven and on earth, the seen and the unseen, thrones, dominions, principalities, authorities; all things have been created through him and for him. So he existed before all things, and through him all things are held together.
>
> Colossians 1:16–17 (WILLIAMS)

Jesus ranks alone. No one compares to him; He has no genuine competitors. He is not just one among chief princes; He is the authority, to whom the chief princes answer. Hence, it is clear that while Michael is among chief princes, Jesus is other than any and so these two cannot be the same person.

Some arguments used to depict Michael as Jesus are like Jude 9:

> Yet Michael the archangel, when contending with the devil he disputed about the body of Moses, durst not bring against him a railing accusation, but said, The Lord rebuke thee.

> Jude 1:9

It is alleged here that since Michael the archangel said to the devil, "the Lord rebuke thee," then that means he was that Lord speaking to the devil! That is what even the Living Bible Translation tried to do, to make Michael the Lord. Hence, Michael the "lord" is said or depicted to be Jesus the Lord. But this is not only false but ridiculous too. If Michael was the alleged Lord, why did he speak on a third-person sense, meaning he was referring to someone other than him? And why did he not just tell the devil straight, "I Michael, the Lord, rebuke thee"? He could not use the first-person pronoun *I* because he was not referring to himself.

Secondly, he knew very well he was not the Lord, and even Satan knew it. In saying *the Lord rebuke thee*, Michael was invoking (appealing to) the name or authority of the Lord, whose he was. At that time, the name *Jesus* had not been given or authenticated for use, hence the use of the word *lord*. Yet that was a common expression then.

Even Moses instructed Aaron in its usage when blessing the Israelites:

> The LORD bless thee, and keep thee: The
> LORD make his face shine upon thee, and
> be gracious unto thee: The LORD lift up his
> countenance upon thee, and give thee peace.
>
> Numbers 6:24–26

Hence, Aaron and his sons blessed the Israelites using the expression "The Lord bless thee and keep thee, or the Lord lift up his countenance upon thee and give thee peace." Would that have meant Aaron or his sons were the Lord? Of course not; that would be ridiculous if we are to interpret that scripture that way. Or further, does it mean when someone tells you the Lord bless you; then the one speaking to you is the Lord? Definitely not.

David too used that expression in Psalms.

> A Psalm of David. The LORD said unto my
> Lord, Sit thou at my right hand, until I make
> thine enemies thy footstool.
>
> Psalm 110:1

The Lord in the above expression was not talking to himself but to another. If we try interpreting this expression "the LORD said unto my Lord" to mean the Lord was talking to himself, then we are to be pitied.

The AMPlified Bible makes it clearer.

> The LORD (God) says to my Lord (the
> Messiah), Sit at My right hand, until I make
> your adversaries Your footstool. [*Matthew*

26:64; *Acts* 2:34; 1 *Corinthians* 15:25; *Colossians* 3:1; *Hebrews* 12:2]

Psalm 110:1 (AMP)

This expression is also found in Zechariah.

And the LORD said unto Satan, The LORD rebuke thee, O Satan; even the LORD that hath chosen Jerusalem rebuke thee: is not this a brand plucked out of the fire?

Zechariah 3:2

The New Revised Standard Version brings out the last part of that verse as, "is not this man a brand plucked from the fire?"

For a clearer understanding of what was taking place here, it is better you read all of Zechariah chapter three. But generally from verse one, we find the prophet given the vision of Joshua the high priest. The high priest was standing before the Angel of the Lord (accepted in the Old Testament to be pre-incarnate Christ) with Satan to his right ready to resist or oppose him; then without a word or explanation to the high priest, the Lord got into intercession on the high priest's behalf—rebuking Satan. Intercession is one of the major distinguishing ministries of Jesus Christ; hence, this Lord who got into intercession was definitely Jesus.

As already explained, he was called the Angel of the Lord, but we see him interceding by invoking the name of another Lord, who is not himself. Thus, when he said *the Lord rebuke thee, Satan*, he did not mean that

that Lord was himself. This becomes clearer as we see him qualifying the word *lord* as the one who had chosen Jerusalem. Why did he do that? He did it so there could be no mistake or confusion as to whom he was referring. The Lord he spoke of who had chosen Jerusalem is known to be the Father; that means it was not himself. Especially in verses seven, the Angel of the Lord clearly tells Joshua that the Lord he is talking about is the Lord of hosts, who is Jehovah Sabaoth.

Hence, the point is that whosoever invokes the name or authority of another is never referring to himself. Therefore, Michael the archangel was not referring to himself as the Lord when he said the Lord rebuke thee.

Secondly, there is also some confusion about Michael from 1 Thessalonians.

> For the Lord himself shall descend from heaven with a shout, with the voice of the archangel, and with the trump of God: and the dead in Christ shall rise first.
>
> 1 Thessalonians 4:16

The proponents of this theory make the above scripture to be understood that the Lord himself will descend with a shout, with the voice of the archangel. That is that the Lord himself is the archangel (Michael) who through his voice will descend from heaven shouting! But the Bible does not say the Lord himself shall descend from heaven shouting, rather that there shall be a shout preceding, going forth ahead of or alongside his descent. It says the Lord himself will descend *with a shout*. With a shout implies accompanied by or coming alongside.

This expression is also found in the Old Testament:

> God is gone up with a shout, the LORD with the sound of a trumpet.
>
> Psalm 47:5

The Good News Bible reads:

> God goes up to his throne. There are shouts of joy and the blast of trumpets, as the LORD goes up.
>
> Psalm 47:5 (GNB)

In fact, some of the newer Bible translations make 1 Thessalonians clearer.

> There will be the shout of command, the archangel's voice, the sound of God's trumpet, and the Lord himself will come down from heaven. Those who have died believing in Christ will rise to life first.
>
> 1 Thessalonians 4:16 (GNB)

> With a loud command and with the shout of the chief angel and a blast of God's trumpet, the Lord will return from heaven. Then those who had faith in Christ before they died will be raised to life.
>
> 1 Thessalonians 4:16 (CEV)

From these readings, it becomes clear that together with that shouting there will also be the voice of the archangel. Or it could be that the archangel(s) will be the one(s) doing the shouting. In the original Greek text, there is no article *the*; therefore, it may be an archangel not "the" archangel, or it will be archangel as a group and not necessarily the single archangel—Michael. It is very important to get this straight here, for it is the reason you will find a number of translations just saying, "for the Lord himself shall descend from heaven…with the voice of an archangel…not the archangel.

If properly understood, this scripture depicts Jesus to be apart from the shouting and the archangel voice. He is only party to the whole scenario by the fact that it will all be about him; He is the one descending with that group.

In fact, commenting on this, Albert Barnes explains, *with a shout* thus: The word here used (*keleusma*) does not elsewhere occur in the New Testament. It properly means a "cry" of excitement, or of urging on; an outcry, clamor, or shout, as of sailors at the oar, or of soldiers rushing to battle, or of a multitude of people, like hunters to their dogs. And in today's language, it would be a shout of fans cheering their best team. It does not mean here that the Lord would himself make such a shout but that he would be attended with it; that is, with a multitude who would lift up their voice like that of an army rushing to the conflict.

Jesus will be coming to receive his very own. When the bridegroom (Matthews 25:1–13) finally arrived at midnight, there was a cry, "behold the bridegroom cometh," but it was not the groom himself who made that cry! There were those in his delegation who were suited for that kind of purpose. In accord with prearranged functions, they were to make certain preprogrammed noises to alert the bridal side of their arrival. Even as the head of descent from heaven (coming as King of Kings and the Bridegroom) Jesus himself will not do the shouting. There are those in his entourage, specifically ordained for that function.

Therefore, if the archangel will shout or his voice will be heard within that entourage of Christ's descent, then how can he be the bridegroom?

From the Jewish traditions, the bridegrooms never shouted when they went for their brides. A glimpse into the ancient oriental wedding procession can bring this out clearly.

Such a procession began from the groom's home with the groom personally accompanied by friends, musicians, and singers. Amongst the friends were his stewards known as bridegroom companion or friend of the bridegroom, who in some cases acted as the governor to make sure all things went as planned (John 2). This bridegroom's friend could be one or many individuals depending on the status of the groom. When the groom's entourage neared the bride's home, the governor or one of the friends of the groom would signal the designated singer or person to give a lead shout of joy signaling the groom's arrival. As such, it was not the groom himself shouting. This simply means Michael the archangel, whose voice will be heard, is not Jesus. He is a creature, designated to herald the arrival of Jesus the bridegroom.

Thus far, we have observed that Michael appealed to a higher authority than himself when he rebuked Satan in the name of the Lord. Whereas, indeed, Jesus is that Lord who Michael appealed to when confronted with Satan.

Another distinct example refuting this notion of Michael being Jesus is that during one of the theophanic appearances of Christ in the Old Testament (Daniel 10), it was Michael and his team who came to the rescue of the pre-incarnate Christ. If Michael was Jesus, how could he come to rescue himself? The story involved here is that when Daniel was in prayer and fasting for three weeks, on the twenty first day he lifted up his eyes and saw a man clothed in linen, whose loins were girded with fine gold of Uphaz. He saw a man, not an angel. Sometimes people mix this up and think it is talking about Gabriel, but it is not.

A careful look will tell you that here Daniel is now talking of a different personality, because Gabriel came to Daniel first during the third year of Belshazzar's reign. Secondly, he came to him in the first year of the reign of Darius.

However, it was a number of years later during the third year of the reign of Cyrus that the encounter in chapter ten took place. It was not a continuation or one and the same thing with what Daniel saw in chapter nine; these were two totally different encounters with a number of years in between. The incident in chapter nine involved Gabriel while the one in chapter ten involved a man (theophanic appearance of Christ) with a beryl-like body.

Daniel called this man of chapter ten *Lord*, and the man did not deny that he was (Daniel 10:17, 19). If he was just an angel, he would have definitely corrected Daniel by saying what angels usually say in such situations, words like "I am just a fellow servant as you; I am not the Lord," but he did not, thereby accepting the designation *Lord*. Thus, we can deduce from this that he did not correct Daniel because he was indeed the Lord.

This was what is called an open vision, where people see things clearly as they are. There is no symbolism or obscurity in what one sees. Daniel saw this man clearly and as real as you are now seeing the pages of this book. It was the awe about that man that made Daniel fall into a trance. And the man began to explain to him what had transpired behind the scenes. He told Daniel how he was sent from heaven in answer to Daniel's prayers the very first day he had begun praying. But it took that long for him to get to Daniel, because of some spiritual conflicts in the heavenlies. He informed Daniel that a prince of Persia—a demonic spirit (strong man) over Persia—had hindered his immediate delivery of the message—some very important revelations concerning Israel and God's intentions. He only then managed to do it because the heavenly warriors under Michael came and secured him free passage to the earthly realm.

> But the prince of the kingdom of Persia withstood me one and twenty days: but, lo, Michael, one of the chief princes, came to

help me; and I remained there with the kings
of Persia.

Daniel 10:13

The New International Version brings it out even
better:

But the prince of the Persian kingdom resisted
me twenty-one days. Then Michael, one of
the chief princes, came to help me, because I
was detained there with the king of Persia.

Daniel 10:13 (NIV)

How then could Michael be Jesus when he came
to help him out? These two personalities, Jesus and
Michael, cannot be the same person. Michael is an
angel, a created being, an agent of Jesus Christ and not
the Christ himself.

13. *Do Angels wear shoes, and what is the nature of their
apparel?*

Answer: I do not think angels wear shoes. Shoes are
worn by humans for:

    a. Protection (safety)

    b. Comfort and beauty (including cleanliness)

    c. Status

What would angels be protected from warranting their putting on shoes? Natural elements: harsh

weather, thorns, rocks, and the rest are nonexistent in their realm. And as to comfort and beauty, I am not sure if they require that from shoes. Concerning status, I personally do not think angels are after status but are only after serving and drawing attention to God. However, if they were to wear shoes, then theirs would be quite different from ours. Such shoes would be spirit shoes, for angels are spirit beings and cannot put on material shoes. Nevertheless, if this question is in regard to when they appear on earth, I should think they would appear with shoes on their feet so as not to be any different from the humans, whose form they take.

Coming to the nature of their garments, I believe their garments are not like our earthly clothes that we take off and put on. In their realm it seems a person has one garment throughout. This we glean from when Daniel saw the pre-incarnate Christ; and later after several thousands of years, John the revelator also saw the same Christ, but he still looked the same. This shows that in that realm clothing is possibly not changed regularly as is done on earth. I think the reason for this could be that your clothing in that celestial realm is part of your being. The Apostle Paul intimates that we shall be clothed with our heavenly housing—our body, which is in heaven.

> For we know that if our earthly house of this tabernacle were dissolved, we have a building of God, a house not made with hands, eternal in the heavens.
>
> For in this we groan, earnestly desiring to

be clothed upon with our house which is from heaven: If so be that being clothed we shall not be found naked.

For we that are in this tabernacle do groan, being burdened: not for that we would be unclothed, but clothed upon, that mortality might be swallowed up of life.

2 Corinthians 5:1–4

Our earthly bodies are our housing here; however, we are not clothed with them. We clothe them separately. But Paul assures us that we will be clothed with that new heavenly housing. That means we shall be fitted with it as our covering housing. It will be part of our beings as well as our covering and not just something we can put on or off. In the above text Paul says that that housing or covering is eternal, meaning it is not changed at all. That gives the impression that an apparel, garment, or clothing within that celestial realm is not some piece of material one throws over their body but is a part of their being. Therefore, I believe the angelic attires are also part of their beings.

14. *Some people claim there are large parts of the Bible that are silent on angels or in which they were conspicuously absent as proof that angels do not exist. Why was it so, and does those prove there are no angels?*

Answer: The Bible does not say all things all the times or in all its pages; in some instances it just mentions some things once. In fact, there are some things the Bible does not even mention at all. But just because the Bible does not mention or talk about some thing does not disprove its existence. The fact that some parts of the Bible do not talk about angels does not prove or disprove anything about them. It does not mean there are no or were no angels then; since their creation, the angels have always existed more so in their realm. Hence, even if they did not appear to or interact with humans much of the prophets' period, they still existed.

But in portions of the Bible where it is silent about them, it could be that there was nothing noteworthy of the angelic ministry and God did not inspire any of those prophets to write or say anything about them. Otherwise, if there was something to be noted, God would have moved upon the prophets to write it down. Since there is nothing much on them in those portions, we can presume that God did not have anything on them for his people.

Or it can also be said that such times could be those when God concentrated his personal and direct involvement with his people through the prophets and priests without involving his heavenly messengers. And so the records in those portions of the Bible are much more on God's own involvement with the people through the ministry of the prophets and priests without the angelic appearances except with prophets like Isaiah, Jeremiah, Ezekiel, Daniel, and others.

But it has also been suggested that most of the prophetic and priestly offices of then were thought to be opposed to the angelic doctrine as they supposed that it infringed on and degraded God's absolute divinity.

It is supposed they saw no need in such intermediaries between God and the world based on their perception of the doctrine of divine immanence. God was understood to be the King of kings, the sovereign of the whole universe and did not need anyone to supplement or complement his rule. Thus, to think that he needed help to run the universe was just not compatible with that understanding. Therefore, it is thought some of them did not talk or record anything about angels as they presumed that doing so is degrading to God. But those are just conjectures.

Most importantly, like we have stated earlier, angelic functions and appearances are in God's prerogative. Then, since God chose to have no record of them in those sections of the Bible, it would be safe simply to say we do not know the reason for that; otherwise we may be forced into great lengths of speculation trying to clarify something we have not been specifically told.

15. *Where do angels dwell?*

Answer: As has been discussed at length in this book, angels are observed to dwell in God's personal presence according to various scriptural references (Luke 1:19, 26–27; Matthew 18:10). God is both omnipresent and specifically present, and it is his specific presence that has his personal presence. But we are not told what that presence looks like or how it is built or even if it is built at all; not even its geographical location, but it is the angels abode. However, no one can point at it saying it is here or there; it has no physical location. Hence, if the question is about some physical location, the answer is we do not know the location of the angels' dwelling.

16. *Some angels have names. Can you explain the origin of that and if the names have any significance?*

Answer: In the Bible, there are only two angels referred to by name: the Archangel Michael and Gabriel. This occurred much later in the history of the Israelites in what has been termed the postexilic period. Before they went into exile, the Israelites did not seem to denote angels by any specific names. It was in exile that it is presumed they were influenced by the Babylonians' practice of naming their deities as is done to humans.

No sooner did the children of Israel arrive in Babylon than Daniel and the other young men in whom there was no blemish but were well favored and skillful in all wisdom, were given Chaldean names (Daniel 1: 1–7). Daniel was called Belteshazzar, which means "favored or protected by Bel" or "Bel protect the king." But on the other hand it also meant, "lord of the straitened treasure or who lays treasure in secret." The Babylonians had names for every concept they could come up with, and with the Israelites living in their midst it was not long before they also began or adopted the practice. However, they did not borrow angelic names from Babylon but simply adopted their practice of naming deities.

Thus, in their postexilic life they carried that practice and begun calling angels by some descriptive names. For example, Michael's (the archangel) name was thought to have been the angels' war cry against

Satan as it means "who is like God?" Hence, *who is like God,* became the name of the chief angel that led the war against Satan and his hosts. Then there is *Gabriel,* which means "mighty or strong man of God," or as others brings it out, "hero or champion of God." A fact to note here is that their names end in *el,* standing for divinity or God. Their names are tied up with God.

However, other literatures and some extra-biblical texts also list a number of angelic names like Uriel, Raguel, Rafael, Sariel, and so forth; but they are outside the scope of our study on holy angels as they are not in the Bible. Hence, we are not going to say any more than just mention them like that.

As to the significance of the names, I should think they helped people distinguish the angels and be at ease with them whenever they appeared. Names aid in ease of acquaintance and help in building rapport. They also make referencing easy. Before the Israelites adopted the use of angelic names, it was cumbersome and difficult trying to explain an angelic encounter. That was the situation with Samson's parents. An angel appeared to his mother, but she could not properly explain it to her husband (Judges 13:1–18).

> Then the woman came and told her husband, saying, A man of God came unto me, and his countenance was like the countenance of an angel of God, very terrible: but I asked him not whence he was, neither told he me his name.
>
> Judges 13:6

People have always desired a denotation to refer to; Manoah in verse seventeen of Judges 13 asked the angel his name. We observe that even Moses asked the Angel of the Lord for a name to tell the people when they would have asked him who appeared to him. Humans are used to names.

17. *You have taught that angels can take forms other than their natural or supernatural one. Is it only always human form that they take? Does the form they take relate to the message, role, or situation?*

Answer: Biblical revelation teaches that angels can take human form to deliver messages, warning or rescuing people as they may have been sent. The form the Bible reveals they usually take is clearly that of humans, but it does not rule out that angels can take other forms. It is only that we have not been told whether they can or even if they do it.

However, from mythology and some folklore, there abound stories of angels turning into dogs or some other animals. Even some personal angelic encounter stories have such implications, but the Bible is silent on any such forms; and where it is silent we ought to be too.

Hence, we cannot say whether angels can turn into animals or even birds; there is no scriptural support for such innuendos.

Coming to the next part of the question, it is possible that the form the angels take corresponds with where and to whom they are sent. They have to adapt to where they are sent, otherwise they would appear strange to those who should be receiving their message. The angels who were sent into Sodom just went there as any other wayfaring passersby needing assistance that evening (Genesis 19). They did not appear any different from ordinary people the Sodomites were used to.

18. *In most pictorial illustrations and drawings of angels, they are only always depicted as Caucasians, a racial term that in its earlier coinage referred to the "white" race of humankind. How come, and does this mean angels are white?*

Answer: Angels are not physical (human) beings and are neither white nor any color. The depictions usually seen on paintings and drawings of them are just the artists' impressions, which in the earlier centuries spread more from the Western world where people racially were mostly white brown and so forth, but not blacks. Hence, those who drew or pictorially illustrated angels only did it from what they were familiar with, but that does not mean angels are white; they are not.

However, in normal circumstances angels would appear the same color as the people they are sent to, though the Bible is not explicit on that. But we have observed that sometimes their appearances come with brilliance about them that it may even be difficult to judge whether they are white, brown, or black. Thus, we cannot be certain that they are this or that color.

Nonetheless, it is not their color that is important but their message and function. I trust that those who depicted them as *Caucasians* were not intending to make others feel slighted because angels are not depicted in their particular racial colors. However, my statement should not mean there are no people out there prejudiced against other races. There are many, but we should all rejoice because God is not like that; He likes all races the same.

19. *Does God still send angels to people anymore, or did the angelic roles diminish as people got to know God more and more? Does God talk to people directly nowadays, or does he still use the angels?*

Answer: Nothing has changed about God and his human redemptive plans; that means he still sends angels as may be necessary for his divine purposes. If the situations that warrant him sending angels prevail, he will always do so. The Bible does not indicate or even suggest anywhere that he was to stop employing them at any time; angels will always be angels and will keep doing what they were created to do. But their sole purpose is not that of talking to the humans, they are engaged even in other various Kingdom purposes we may not be aware of.

Thus, their roles have not diminished as such and furthermore, as observed above, it was not solely about speaking to people on behalf of God. Their core role mentioned in the Bible is to minister to those who would be heirs of salvation. Human salvation is an ongoing process that has not stopped; hence, there is no way the angelic role could diminish. There is so much ministry going on to the believers though unseen and most of the times unreported.

In terms of God talking to people, the Bible says,

> In the past God spoke to our ancestors many times and in many ways through the prophets, but in these last days he has spoken to us through his Son. He is the one through whom God created the universe, the one whom God has chosen to possess all things at the end.
>
> Hebrews 1:1–2 (GNB)

God talks to the people through his Son and the Word, though sometimes some angels have brought messages to people. But his normal way of talking to humans is his Word and in his Son by the Spirit.

20. *Man was created and given dominion over the earth, does this mean even angels are under man's authority when they come or appear on earth?*

Answer: The first thing to understand here is the fact that though man was given dominion upon the earth, he sold out to the devil and lost it. He no longer rules or is in charge of the earth as God's intention had been. Nonetheless, even if he still would have had the authority over the earth, angels who come or appear on earth would not have been subject to or been under man's authority. I say this because those angels come from a realm of higher jurisdiction; their authority is still above that of man. This is so because the sending authority is far higher above man. This means even the emissaries he sends are considered to be of higher rank than where they are sent.

For instance, if the president of the United States of America sends an envoy to another nation that person carries with him or her, the weight of the authority of the government of the USA. He or she does not become subject to the country he or she is sent, unless he or she willingly chooses to. But then he or she would not be serving the interest of the sending authority or government! Hence, angels do not become subject to man when they are sent to earth.

21. *When Joseph intended to dump Mary (Jesus' mother) when he realized she was pregnant, an angel appeared to him in a dream telling him not to leave her. Does this mean angels know or see the secrets of people's hearts?*

Answer: As previously mentioned angels are not omniscient. They do not know all things, though as beings of a higher realm they possess greater knowledge than man but only what is in their line of service and whatever God may allow them to know.

Hence, when Matthew records,

> Then Joseph her husband, being a just man, and not willing to make her a public example, was minded to put her away privily. But while he thought on these things, behold, the angel of the Lord appeared unto him in a dream, saying, Joseph, thou son of David, fear not to take unto thee Mary thy wife.

> Matthew 1:19–20

It does not mean that this angel knew Joseph's thoughts. The angel spoke to Joseph because Mary needed all the support and encouragement she could get at that juncture. If Joseph misunderstood her, no one else would have understood her, and that would have resulted in her suffering societal rejection and great embarrassment. It would have been very traumatic to her since she already had the baby in her womb. She might even have been accused of promiscuous living and stoned to death, so you can see how precarious her situation was. Then, Joseph was the key to her safety and strength; no one else could do. That is the reason God through his angel had to convince Mr. Joe to stand up to that task, though it involved being misunderstood himself. But he willingly undertook that risk for God's sake.

Nonetheless, that does not mean the angel who came to him knew the secrets of his heart. Angels do not know nor do they see the secrets of peoples' hearts unless God permits them. It is God alone who is a discerner of intents and thoughts of man's heart and he alone knows the secrets of people's hearts.

> And is a discerner of the thoughts and intents of the heart. Neither is there any creature that is not manifest in his sight: but all things are naked and opened unto the eyes of him with whom we have to do.
>
> Hebrews 4:12d-13

Angels do not know the secrets of people's hearts unless God allows them. The Bible seems to confirm this when it asks,

No one can know a person's thoughts except
that person's own spirit, and no one can know
God's thoughts except God's own Spirit.

1 Corinthians 2:11(NLT)

No one, not even angels, know a person's heart
except the person and God or in some cases people with
familiar spirits, but that is a different story for now.

Nonetheless, an angel came to Joseph, not that he
saw or knew Joseph's secrets, but because he was sent.
We must always remember that angels just do not do
their own things; they do not act independent of God.
They only do what they are told or sent to. This means
it was God who, knowing the secrets of Joseph's heart
in plotting to dump Mary sent that angel over to him.
The angel did not just run or fly off to Joseph by his
own initiative. This angel did not respond to the secrets
of Joseph's heart but to the order of God concerning
the same.

22. *What is the angels' mode of communication? How do they
talk if they do at all?*

Answer: As far as angelic communications are concerned, we are not exactly told how they do it. There
have been various arguments that angels speak Hebrew
or claims that it is Chaldean Aramaic. Those who
advance Hebrew as their language argue that angels as
holy beings converse only in the holy tongue, which
they claim is Hebrew. No wonder, in some rabbinic
teachings it was advanced that with the exception of
Gabriel, who was purported to know every language,

the angels were said to be ignorant of Aramaic. But that also was later found to be an assertion from the desire to preserve Hebrew as it was thought to be on its way out, being displaced by Aramaic as the vernacular of the Jews then. Hence, the war of the language has been intense not only then, but even now with others claiming angelic language is Greek. Some also assert it is Latin and so forth. Even recently claims have been made that they speak Arabic. But the Apostle Paul speaking to the Corinthians made reference to the fact that angels have their own language.

> Though I speak with the *tongues of* men and of *angels*.
>
> 1 Corinthians 13:1 (emphasis added)

It is mentioned here that men have their languages and angels do too. All the above mentioned languages are humans' and cannot be the angels.' Thus, all who argue for any of the earthly languages to be the angelic one are definitely wrong. Angels have a tongue or a language of their own, but we are not sure what it is or how it goes. We are not even told how God speaks to them, but somehow he does.

Someone averred that angels are monolingual beings speaking a heavenly tongue not known on earth. However, as for those angels who appear to people on earth, it is recorded they speak just with the human voice and language. That means if an angel appears to a Spaniard, he will speak Spanish. If he appears to a Chinaman, he will speak Chinese and so forth. But that does not then become the angel language. As we have stated, angels have a tongue or a language of their own not known on earth.

23. *Does everyone alive have a guardian angel assigned to them?*

Answer: The idea or teaching of guardian angels is an old darling to many people, being an old doctrine that gained momentum somewhere around fourth century, likely from the patron-angel theory prevalent during those times. It was coined and propagated by those who wanted to motivate people with a sense of divine security thought to have probably started from the Jewish traditions but much later popularized by the Catholic traditions and teachings through the likes of St. Basil.

However, even today people love to hear that they have guardian angels assigned to watch over them; it gives them hope and dispels fear. But it is false as far as the scriptures are concerned. There are no particular angels assigned to hover over people everywhere every time purportedly guarding them. The Bible does not teach such a thing. Angels only attend or minister to people always from God's personal presence.

> And the angel answering said unto him, *I am Gabriel, that stand in the presence of God*; and am sent to speak unto thee, and to show thee these glad tidings.
>
> Luke 1:19 (emphasis added)

The angel in the Scripture above was sent to Zacharias directly from God's presence. He was not hovering over Zacharias' head everywhere Zac went. The angel clearly said he came from God's presence. The same angel a few months later was then sent somewhere else.

> And in the sixth month the angel Gabriel was sent from God unto a city of Galilee, named Nazareth, To a virgin espoused to a man whose name was Joseph, of the house of David; and the virgin's name was Mary.
>
> Luke 1:26–27

Note that the angel had been sent from God. Angels only deliver messages or minister as situations may call for and then immediately return to God's presence. They do not dwell with people; their dwelling place is God's presence. They do not hang around people looking or waiting for some danger so as to show their prowess. Michael was considered the Jewish guardian angel, but did he live always hovering around Israel? Definitely not, he always responded to situations directly from God's presence, where all angels dwell.

Even the denotation *guardian angel* is not a scriptural term but a coinage of those who created it. It signifies these angels to be just guards, yet angels are multi-task creatures. In fact, the notion of them just being guards raises more questions than answers. What are they guarding, and for how long? Is their work only to guard?

When does this work begin: at conception or after birth and if after birth at what age? Supposing other situations arise not related to guarding, does God have to send other angels? And if those others are sent, do they confer with the so-called guardian angels, or does everybody mind their own business? Do these so-called guardian angels ever take leave? Where was Mary's guardian angel if at all she had one when Gabriel appeared to her, and what was it doing then? What happens in accidents and catastrophes? Do guardian angels fail their duties? And many more questions in that line.

Thus, the notion that God assigns people angels who follow them everywhere is false. Consider what the Apostle Paul went through. If God was assigning guardian angels to people, Paul should have qualified. However, he suffered so much especially in the hands of his fellow Jews. Listen as he narrates the things he suffered.

> From the Jews I five times have received forty lashes all but one. Three times I have been beaten with Roman rods, once I have been stoned, three times I have been shipwrecked, once for full four and twenty hours I was floating on the open sea.
> I have served him by frequent travelling, amid dangers in crossing rivers, dangers from robbers; dangers from my own countrymen, dangers from the Gentiles; dangers in the city, dangers in the Desert, dangers by sea, dangers from spies in our midst; with labour and toil,

with many a sleepless night, in hunger and thirst, in frequent fastings, in cold, and with insufficient clothing.

2 Corinthians 11:24–27 (Weymouth)

In terms of angelic protection, where was Paul's guardian angel as he went through his many harrowing experiences? What sort of things should those purported angels be protecting one from if not the kinds that Paul went through? It is clear from Paul's life experiences that he did not depend on guardian angels but on his Lord who loved him and gave himself for him. In the midst of his experiences, Paul stated that he knew whom he had believed: the victoriously risen and ever living Lord Jesus. Paul depended on Jesus and not on the angels. Angels served him, but he did not look to them; his gaze was upon Jesus, the author and finisher of his faith (Hebrews 12:2).

However, we can say that *guardian* angels (to continue using the term) are those God has given specific charge with the protection or guarding his people at specific points in time. The Bible says, "for he shall give his angels charge over thee, to keep thee in all thy ways" (Psalm 91:11). This, God does as situations may call for, but he does not assign those angels to stick with people throughout. Angels only serve in various ways God commands them but then return to his presence.

Angels whether to guard or guide are always dispatched from God's personal presence whenever the need arises and are only available to his people for a specific time.

Are not the angels all ministering spirits (servants) sent out in the service [*of God
for the assistance*] of those who are to inherit
salvation?

Hebrews 1:14 (AMP)

What are the angels, then? They are spirits
who serve God and are sent by him to help
those who are to receive salvation.

Hebrews 1:14 (GNB)

However, if an angel is assigned to us (talking about
believers) as guardians, then what becomes of the
promise of Jesus that he will always be with us?

For he hath said, I will never leave thee, nor
forsake thee.

Hebrews 13:5

Does Jesus come in the form of an angel? How about
the greater one that is supposed to be in us according
to 1 John 4:4?

Furthermore, the Scriptures instruct us to rely on
the indwelling Spirit of God. Why is an external guardian angel necessary when the King of glory himself is
supposedly resident in a believer? The guardian angel
teaching makes a lot of scriptures lose their meaning
and practical applications. Moreover, the Bible clearly
states that believers are kept by the power of God
through faith and not by angels!

Blessed be the God and Father of our Lord Jesus Christ, which according to his abundant mercy hath begotten us again unto a lively hope by the resurrection of Jesus Christ from the dead, To an inheritance incorruptible, and undefiled, and that fadeth not away, reserved in heaven for you, Who are kept by *the power of God* through faith unto salvation ready to be revealed in the last time. Wherein ye greatly rejoice, though now for a season, if need be, ye are in heaviness through manifold temptations.

1 Peter 1:3–6(emphasis added)

While speaking on this, Paul intimates that God has provided an armor for Christians protection and use in warfare (Ephesians 6:10–19). He does not tell them to call on God for angels!

James also admonishes believers saying,

Submit yourselves therefore to God. Resist the devil, and he will flee from you.

James 4:7

James tells the believers to resist the devil and the devil will flee from them; he does not tell them to wait for an angel to chase the devil away. The devil and his cohorts are already defeated. Man does not need angels to keep him from demonic attacks; he only needs the understanding that Jesus has already dealt a blow to the devil and then walk in the authority of that understanding. Knowing and applying such a truth will set him free from the fear of the devil.

It has clearly been stated that the devil is a defeated foe; Jesus defeated him openly hanging up high between the heavens and the earth, by which act he set us free not to fear the devil any more.

> You were dead because of your sins and because your sinful nature was not yet cut away. Then God made you alive with Christ, for he forgave all our sins. He canceled the record of the charges against us and took it away by nailing it to the cross. In this way, he disarmed the spiritual rulers and authorities. He shamed them publicly by his victory over them on the cross.
>
> Colossians 2:13–15(NLT).

Thus, man does not need angels to help him in regard to the devil; he just needs to take authority over the devil in Jesus' name, in submission to God. This is important for believers if their faith will ever be exercised. But remember man's major problem is not all the wicked spirits supposedly targeting him but the evil within him. Without God to change man's sinful nature, there is no hope for him even if ten thousand angels were to be set directly above him! Someone added that as Christians we must understand that Christ has already won the victory for us. He has defeated the devil and his evil ones. Therefore, the ground for our victory over them is only when we are found in union with Christ and not by some angelic protection!

24. *Can you then please explain Matthews* 18:10 *that states, "take heed that ye despise not one of these little ones; for I say unto you, That in heaven their angels do always behold the face of my Father which is in heaven?"*

Answer: A proper understanding of this text is needed, as it is one of the verses most guardian-angels theorists base their teachings on. Traditionally it is purported to mean that Jesus said that little children each have their guardian angel, which appears before God daily or frequently on their behalves. However, that is incorrect; it makes Jesus' subject of speech "the little children," whereas, his subject was those who believed in him, his disciples.

To properly understand this, we need to read from the very first verse. In verse one, there arose bickering and disputing among Jesus' disciples as to who was greatest among them. But instead of Jesus pronouncing any of them great, He, in verse two called a little child and set him in their midst. And in verse three he began speaking to them using the little child as his pictorial illustration, for their ease of understanding.

> And said, Verily I say unto you, Except ye be converted, and become as little children, ye shall not enter into the kingdom of heaven.
>
> Matthews 18:3

He gave them a profound teaching on servant leadership, based on the qualities of a child's lifestyle. He was not talking about the *little child* or *children per se* but used that to illustrate the state children, though not sinless, are in. Such is the state of assumed innocence or clear conscience, humility, and teach-ability, non-assuming, destitute of vain ambitions and pride, not vainly envious of others, and so forth. Jesus was teaching his disciples not to despise each other while thinking highly of themselves or being convinced of their own supremacy. He rather wanted them to be turned around (converted) from their prideful disputing and jostling to take on childlike spirits.

He set that little child in their midst and began teaching them referring to him in his lesson, especially in verse four; "Whosoever therefore shall humble himself as this little child, the same is greatest in the kingdom of heaven." Then in verse five he said, "And whoso shall receive one such little child in my name receiveth me." It is here he lastly referred to that little child. He then changed the subject in verse six, from that little child to "little ones who believe in him," his followers. He said, "But whoso shall offend one of these little ones which believe in me ... "

When he said, "these little ones," he did not mean little children or the little child. The subject had changed from that little child to "these little ones." It changed from singular to plural as Jesus was then talking of his disciples and not children. He was talking of the little one who believed in him. They were little in the sense that in the world's eyes they were lowly people. The world considered them base and of no account, in fact contemptible in the world's estimation, though persons of grace and usefulness to God.

However, they were believers being taught how to manifest childlike spirit. How do we know they were believers? Verse six has told us through the phrase, "of these little ones which believe in me." Little children and infants are not capable of making informed decisions to place their faith in Jesus Christ. Hence, Jesus could not be talking of them when he said "these little ones." This reference did not refer to little children or infants but to those lowly ones who had specifically believed in Jesus. It is the same phrase in verse ten.

Therefore, in verse ten Jesus was not teaching that each little child has a special angel who appears in God's presence for them. The angels were for *the little ones* who believed in Jesus and not for the little children. It is important to understand this; because it is the point of confusion where people presume the reference "little ones" talks about the little children. It does not; those little ones were those who had believed in and received Jesus as their Lord and savior. They were not little children but little ones. Having believed in Jesus as Lord and savior, they were among the heirs of salvation, and according to Hebrews 1:14 there were angels in God's presence ready to minister to them.

In Matthews 18:10, those angels are referred to as their angels, though not as assigned specifically to each one of them. They are their angels not in a personal sense but corporately. The words *their angels* are used in a general sense. They mean angels or a group of angels who involve or are concerned with the affairs of those who are or would be heirs of salvation. The sense in which the words are used can be found in other general references like following the skirmishes in that neighborhood *their leaders* called for a meeting between the warring groups. It does not mean each person within that neighborhood had a specific leader assigned to him or her. The reference "their leaders" is in a general sense; it is a group of leaders, as is the reference "their angels." These were angels in God's presence as ministering spirits ready for ministry to the heirs of salvation.

As such, these little ones who had believed in Jesus were saved or heirs of salvation. For that reason, they had angels readily available in God's presence to minister to them whenever God deemed necessary. Hebrews 1:14 says those angels only minister to the heirs of salvation when they are sent. This means such angels are not supposedly hovering over those little ones but are always beholding God's face. In other words, those angels are mostly in God's personal presence in heavenly places unless they are sent. How then are those angels guarding those little ones if they are always before God in heaven? Are they really guardians?

If properly understood, this verse does not teach the existence of guardian angels over every human being alive or even over the little children or infants. However, it informs us of the great concern and care God has for and takes over those who accept his grace through his Son Jesus; He has availed angelic hosts to minister to them as may be necessary, but not to hover over them. Thus, it is false and presumptuous to interpret that verse to promote the guardian-angel theory.

25. *Do angels respond to prayers?*

Answer: No, it is not true that angels respond to prayers; they only respond to God's orders or commands. Furthermore, we pray to God not to or through the angels! Christians are never anywhere told or even given the slightest hint that they can pray to or even address the angels rather than God. Different religious groups may have that option within their practices, but Christians can and should only pray to God.

Even our Lord Jesus inferred that angels can only come (be released or sent) by asking the Father. He did not say, "Don't you know I can order the angels or even pray to and have twelve legions attend to me?" His question, "thinkest thou that I cannot now *pray* to my Father, and he shall presently give me more than twelve legions of angels?" (Matthews 26:53, emphasis added) clearly shows this. When we pray to God he is the only one who as may be necessary can dispatch angels to attend to our various needs.

Though in the earlier centuries there were thoughts and teachings propagating that there was a special class of angels that listened to prayers and praises, and that at the end of every worship service, they gathered up the devotions and prayers of God's people and presented them to God. But those were just people's own make-believe; there are no such thoughts in the Scriptures. God hears directly from the mouth of the petitioners or the worshippers.

Thus, God is the one answering prayers when an angel is sent; it is not the angel responding to someone's prayers! This is well illustrated further by the Apostle Peter's case in Acts 12. Peter was arrested after Herod killed

James the brother of John and saw it pleased the Jews. But the church then did not sit helpless. They united and joined together in earnest prayers to God concerning Peter.

That's when King Herod got it into his head to go after some of the church members. He murdered James, John's brother. When he saw how much it raised his popularity ratings with the Jews, he arrested Peter—all this during Passover Week, mind you—and had him thrown in jail, putting four squads of four soldiers each to guard him. He was planning a public lynching after Passover.

All the time that Peter was under heavy guard in the jailhouse, the church prayed for him most strenuously. Then the time came for Herod to bring him out for the kill. That night, even though shackled to two soldiers, one on either side, Peter slept like a baby. And there were guards at the door keeping their eyes on the place. Herod was taking no chances!

Suddenly there was an angel at his side and light flooding the room. The angel shook Peter and got him up: "Hurry!" The handcuffs fell off his wrists. The angel said, "Get dressed. Put on your shoes." Peter did it. Then, "Grab your coat and let's get out of here."

Peter followed him, but didn't believe it was really an angel—he thought he was dreaming. Past the first guard and then the second, they came to the iron gate that led into the city. It swung open before them on its own, and they were out on the street, free as the breeze. At the first intersection the angel left him, going his own way.

That's when Peter realized it was no dream. "I can't believe it—this really happened! The Master sent his angel and rescued me from Herod's vicious little production and the spectacle the Jewish mob was looking forward to." Still shaking his head, amazed, he went to Mary's house, the Mary who was John Mark's mother. The house was packed with praying friends.

Acts 12:1–12 (MSG)

It is true the church earnestly prayed to God for Peter and an angel was sent to rescue him. Yet that angel came not in response to the church's prayers but simply because God specifically must have sent him. We do not know what their exact prayers were, but in response, God saw it fit that only an angel could be the appropriate answer then. It is not prayers that move angels but God's direct commands.

Bless the LORD, ye his angels, that excel in strength, that do his commandments, hearkening unto the voice of his word.

Psalm 103:20

There it is, the Scriptures declaring clearly that angels move only at the command of God's Word or voice. There can be no better way to summarize all we have been saying on this than that, *angels do His commandments, hearkening unto the voice of His word.*

Angels do not listen to your prayers, since those prayers are directed to God and not to them; they have no business meddling in them. They only listen to God. In fact, this fact dispels some of those New Age theories that you can talk to or direct or even command "your angel." There is no word for such ideas in the Bible.

If one can converse with or even command an angel at his own initiative, then that must be some other angel and not God's. And such disguised angels are very much around; however, you cannot realize who they are from the outset. In fact, such involvements begin as though those purported angels are the real angels of light. But down the involvement you will not even know when you are being led astray. Those purported angels begin by developing a good rapport with you to the point you completely trust yourself to them, only to be taken advantage of in the end. Those beings masquerading as angels are in reality demon spirits, or familiar spirits.

Therefore, one of the ways to avoid such traps is to be scripturally sound. Measure all things by the standard of God's Word. Shun messages and communications made to appeal to your emotions and intellect only. One thing for sure is that God's angels do not listen to prayers; they only listen to God!

26. *Roughly guessing, in what situations is God likely to send an angel to someone?*

Answer: Wow, it would be difficult if not impossible to know what God would do when and how, because no one directs God. The Bible even says that no one knows the things of God except his Spirit. Hence, I do not purport to know when God might send someone an angel. However, a keen study of the angelic appearances shows a pattern that could point us to the answer. But before we look at that pattern, it is important that we understand that angelic appearances to people are some of God's answers to those specific individuals at those points in time.

However, in most cases God uses humans to reach out to or be answers to other people's needs. People are God's answers to your needs. When we petition God concerning our various needs, his answers do not drop from heaven. He mostly uses other people as means to the answers we so needed. God mostly uses humans to touch, bless, or reach other humans. Nevertheless, in situations that are impossible for man, God then sends angels. And that is the pattern. Let's sample a few of the angelic appearances recorded in the Bible, beginning with the appearance to Gideon in Judges 6.

> And there came an angel of the LORD, and sat under an oak which was in Ophrah, that pertained unto Joash the Abi-ezrite: and his son Gideon threshed wheat by the winepress, to hide it from the Midianites. And the angel of the LORD appeared unto him, and said unto him, The LORD is with thee, thou mighty man of valor.
> And Gideon said unto him, Oh my Lord,

if the LORD be with us, why then is all this
befallen us? and where be all his miracles
which our fathers told us of, saying, Did not
the LORD bring us up from Egypt? but now
the LORD hath forsaken us, and delivered us
into the hands of the Midianites.

And the LORD looked upon him, and said,
Go in this thy might, and thou shalt save
Israel from the hand of the Midianites: have
not I sent thee? And he said unto him, Oh my
Lord, wherewith shall I save Israel? behold,
my family is poor in Manasseh, and I am the
least in my father's house. And the LORD said
unto him, Surely I will be with thee, and thou
shalt smite the Midianites as one man.

Judges 6:11–16

This story continues on up to the end of that chapter. However, because of the situation the Israelites were
in, impoverished, demoralized, and hiding in caves, it
seemed difficult from the human standpoint to find
anyone who could have inspired Gideon to faith. As
such, that which was impossible with man, God in his
prerogative decided that only an angel could do. Hence,
the Angel of the Lord was sent to Gideon.

Look also at the case of Zacharias, the father of
John the Baptizer.

A certain priest named Zacharias, of the course
of Abijah: and his wife was of the daughters
of Aaron, and her name was Elisabeth. And

they were both righteous before God, walking in all the commandments and ordinances of the Lord blameless. And they had no child, because that Elisabeth was barren, and they both were now well stricken in years. And it came to pass, that while he executed the priest's office before God in the order of his course,

And there appeared unto him an angel of the Lord standing on the right side of the altar of incense. And when Zacharias saw him, he was troubled, and fear fell upon him. But the angel said unto him, Fear not, Zacharias: for thy prayer is heard; and thy wife Elisabeth shall bear thee a son, and thou shalt call his name John. And thou shalt have joy and gladness; and many shall rejoice at his birth.

And Zacharias said unto the angel, Whereby shall I know this? for I am an old man and my wife well stricken in years. And the angel answering said unto him, I am Gabriel, that stand in the presence of God; and am sent to speak unto thee, and to show thee these glad tidings. And, behold, thou shalt be dumb, and not able to speak, until the day that these things shall be performed, because thou believest not my words, which shall be fulfilled in their season.

Luke 1:5b-8, 11–14, 18–20

It was impossible even for Zacharias' fellow priests to convince him that he would bear John. He might have been convinced in his mind that it was over for him. Probably he did not even like thinking about how he had yearned and prayed for a son. It was impossible from the human standpoint even to stir up his mind in that direction. As such, God sent him an angel. The story is the same even in regard to Mary the mother of our Lord. Only an angel could do. Even the rescue of Peter from jail in Acts 12 no person would have done it without serious and unfavorable repercussions to them or their families. Only an angel could do it. Hence, I submit that God is likely to send someone an angel only when there is no possibility of employing human agents. And such situations only God can judge.

27. *How would you explain the verse that says, "the angel of the* LORD *encampeth round about them that fear him, and delivereth them" (Psalm 34:7)?*

Answer: This verse simply tells what angels do when they are sent to God's children. They encamp; this carries the thought of "surrounding as with a hedge." When the said person (believer) is surrounded as with a hedge, that acts as a barrier to the enemy's attacks at that point in time and hence, results in deliverance from the enemy. Or it may also mean that after surrounding the believer with their presence; dependent on the nature of the situation, the angel may then deliver, rescue, and lead to safety that particular individual. This was the case when Peter was delivered from Herod's jail (Acts 12:1–10). The common thought people attach to this verse is that angels come and pitch tents or a camp of some sort on the individual's life, becoming the much propagated guardian angel. Yet that is not consistent with Scriptures. Scriptures show that angels belong in God's personal presence and only come to minister to people as they are sent.

28. *There is also an idea that there is going to be increased angelic activities in the end times. What would result in this, and how true is it?*

Answer: Angelic activities have been going on every day; it is only that a lot of it is never reported. But to say there is going to be an increase in these activities is kind of trying to say God is going to change his *modus oparendi*. It is like saying he is going to speed up the pace of doing his businesses. Yet that is not true; God has his own calendar, not even known to the angels themselves, for all of it is within the counsel of his own will.

Furthermore, he is never in any sort of a hurry. We also need to note that angelic activities in actual sense are God's activities, as he is the one who sets the agenda for the angelic activities. It is true as end times are concerned there is much that is expected to take place in the world circles. Some may involve direct angelic activities while others may not.

Yet everything will just function or run as God has purposed them from before. I think there would not be any increase or decrease at all in what God is doing. It would only be an increase in the awareness of such activities as may have been the case on the first advent of Christ. There seemed to have been no angelic activities for a period of several hundred years. Then suddenly within God's program for the incarnation, the heaven was a buzz, and it appeared there was an increase in angelic activities.

There was an angel sent to Zacharias to announce the birth of Christ's forerunner. A few months later, the same was dispatched to Mary in Nazareth. Yet in reality, this was not an increase from God's standpoint, maybe from man's viewpoint. It might then be that at Christ's next advent too there may be a repeat of such activities. For when finally he comes back to earth, there will definitely be a stir among the angels, with some in his entourage, others sent to gather the elect and bind the chaff ready for destruction.

From the book of Revelation, we understand that God's angels will be directly involved with the various functions and judgments on earth. In fact, in that book we read of angelic hosts given charge over various elements like angel of the waters, angels in charge of the wind, and so on. Hence, it might be within the context of the book of Revelation that suggests there will be increased angelic activities. However, all that is not necessarily an increase in the angelic activities but only an increase in the awareness of them.

I believe there is so much that goes on within the angelic realms, even right now that we have not been made aware of. Since we are unawares, we think that nothing goes on, and when we glimpse into what will happen later from the book of Revelation we conclude it will be an increase. Had we not been informed, we would not have had such conclusions, yet the angelic activities would still have gone on.

Still, what people refer to as an increase in angelic activities might turn out to be the increase in reporting such encounters, bringing an awareness of them.

Nevertheless, there is a sense in which New Age groups use this phrase to mean an increase from man's viewpoint, which is unscriptural. Otherwise, this statement may just be another popular Christian cliché of the moment.

29. *The Scriptures say that God sent an angel or angels to fight for and guard the Israelites in their journey to the Promised Land. What could be the reason for this and how come he did it only to the Israelites?*

Answer: God's eternal plan of redemption and reconciliation was bound up with Israel as his choice vehicle then that carried the *transcendent seed of woman*, who was the center of that entire plan. And in that plan is bound up the very glory of God ready to be revealed at the consummation of his magnificent and eternal purpose. Therefore, he instituted an age-long program by which he was to establish his eternal purposes involving humankind and creation.

This he did by choosing the Hebrew race through Abraham out of all the others, and he wanted to make it a *magnum opus* to humanity. It was going to be an example to the rest of humanity of the goodness of involvements with the living God, his unending mercies, inexhaustible grace and forgiveness and longsuffering patience in restoring them even after they rebelled from him.

Thus, God was going to involve and interact with them and work himself into them so they could well portray him to the whole world. It was through and by them that God's transcendent seed, the only begotten Son of the Father, sometimes referred to as the seed of woman or seed of Abraham was to come.

> And I will put enmity between thee and the woman, and between thy seed and her seed; he shall crush thy head, and thou shalt crush his heel.
>
> Genesis 3:15 (DARBY)

> Now to Abraham and his seed were the promises made. He saith not, And to seeds, as of many; but as of one, And to thy seed, which is Christ.
>
> Galatians 3:16

This promised seed contained within him all that God had purposed to bring about and he was to come through the Israelites. For this reason, the Israelites were the apple of God's eyes then, and he could not let anything interfere with his reconciliation program that was to be set rolling through and from them. He thus set them apart for himself.

> Now therefore, if ye will obey my voice indeed, and keep my covenant, then ye shall be a peculiar treasure unto me above all people: for all the earth is mine: And ye shall be unto me a kingdom of priests, and a holy nation.
>
> Exodus 19:5–6

Good News Bible says,

> Now, if you will obey me and keep my covenant, you will be my own people. The whole earth is mine, but you will be my chosen people, a people dedicated to me alone, and you will serve me as priests.
>
> Exodus 19:5–6 (GNB)

Furthermore, when the Israelites left Egypt, they were just a bunch of pastoralists turned slave brick makers and not trained soldiers; whereas, the people whose lands they were to pass through had experienced, well-trained, and equipped warriors. The Israelites even had no weapons: spears, bows and arrows, shields, and chariots. They only had silver and gold they had acquired from the Egyptians and then their livestock.

They were just a group of freed slaves who got a break from their back-breaking brick-making job for the first time in a long time. They did not envision themselves fighting as that had not been part of their lives. They were mostly glad to be free then and looked to God for the rest of their lives. Hence, God had to take care of them in all things. They were ill prepared for any fight, and certainly the odds were against them in every turn in terms of military preparedness. Moreover, God did not intend for them to fight immediately after they left Egypt peradventure their hearts would have desired to return to Egypt.

> And it came to pass, when Pharaoh had let the people go, that God led them not through

the way of the land of the Philistines, although that was near; for God said, Lest peradventure the people repent when they see war, and they return to Egypt.

Exodus 13:17

However, he had promised to protect them when he pledged that he would bring them *out* of Egypt to bring them *into h*is promise.

And the LORD said, I have surely seen the affliction of my people which are in Egypt, and have heard their cry by reason of their taskmasters; for I know their sorrows; And I am come down to deliver them out of the hand of the Egyptians, and to bring them up out of that land unto a good land and a large, unto a land flowing with milk and honey.

Exodus 3:7–8a

Therefore, having pledged he would take care of them, it behooved God to do just that involving even fighting for them, since they were disadvantaged compared to their enemies. Such interventions involved the sending of angels and other divinely inspired moves because in some of their situations no human instrumentality could have helped them. And this was only to them then as the promised seed-bearers and as the firstfruit that the Lord intended to use to bring about the unfolding of his divine plans touching the rest of creation. The Bible says,

> Israel was holiness unto the LORD, and the
> *firstfruits* of his increase: all that devour him
> shall offend; evil shall come upon them, saith
> the LORD.

> Jeremiah 2:3(emphasis added)

Thus, any people who stood contrary to Israel did so against the Lord God, and so he took charge of their protection unto bringing them into their inheritance. Hence, it was the nation of Israel alone then that though undeserving received God's divine special favors.

30. *What can one do to see an angel?*

Answer: There are some popular teachings today encouraging people not only to seek to see "their" angels, but to know them as well! However, it is important to remember that none of us has "our" angels. All angels are God's and only serve people as God assigns. For example, Mary could not claim Gabriel to be her angel just because he brought her a message from God. But that is what some folks would have us believe, that any angel sent to you then becomes your angel. Such an idea is foreign to biblical revelation.

Angels are not in the power of man to switch on and off as he may like. You cannot just decide you want to see angels and command or demand to see them. Even praying to see them may not serve any useful purpose in God's plans for you. If God deems it necessary to have you encounter an angel, he is the one to send them. But just praying to see an angel is like telling God to satisfy your curiosity.

Furthermore, God has not told any of us to seek to know or see angels. He would rather that we seek to get to know him. His intention and desire is that mankind should have a deep personal relationship with him, through Christ Jesus his Son. But not that we should seek to develop relationships with angels; angels are just mere agents he employs in the function and servicing of his will and purposes. As we have said all through in this book, angels are in God's power, and he alone decides where, when, and to whom the angels can be sent. And that must be something purposeful within his eternal plans, not just to satisfy someone's curiosity. God only works in all things in accord to his divine purposes.

> In whom also we have obtained an inheritance, being predestinated according to the purpose of him who worketh all things after the counsel of his own will.
>
> Ephesians 1:11

The Amplified Bible reads thus:

> In him we also were made [*God's*] heritage (portion) and we obtained an inheritance; for we had been foreordained (chosen and appointed beforehand) in accordance with his purpose, Who works out everything in agreement with the counsel and design of his [*own*] will.
>
> Ephesians 1:11 (AMP)

If it is within his purposed will for you to encounter or see an angel, then he will definitely send one your way. But there is nothing anyone can do to qualify to see an angel. It is not the level of your spirituality or anything about you that can make you see angels. There have been testimonies of young children encountering angels, yet they are not the most spiritual. Seeing an angel is in God's power because angels' movements are in God's prerogative. All the people who encountered, saw, or were ministered to by angels had nothing to do with their appearing in the first place. Mary, Gideon, and others did nothing to make the angels appear to them. They just lived their lives consistently before God, and from his own counsel, he sent them those angels. As such, the thing one can do, though not necessarily to make angels appear to them, is to live consistently before God. Remember, we have not been called to live by sight, including seeing angels, but by faith in God and his Word.

However, people just desire angelic encounters so they can brag to their friends how special they think they are. But seeing or encountering an angel does not in any way make anyone a special person. It does not even enhance or increase one's spiritual stature. Others also think that by seeing an angel their faith will grow leaps and bounds, but that also is false. Faith does not come by sight, even seeing an angel, but by the Word of God. The Bible clearly teaches that:

> So then faith cometh by hearing, and hearing by the word of God.
>
> Romans 10:17

However, encountering a holy angel may definitely have some effects on your life, as it did in Gideon's. But after the experience wears off, you will still have to live by faith. For the same reason, Paul admonishes us to let the Word of Christ dwell richly in us. The richer the Word dwells in you, the greater your faith shall be as God's truth becomes more real to you. Our desires should not just be the seeing of angels, but more so being in a proper relationship with God himself and that we may grow in our daily walk with him.

It is of no spiritual benefit to anyone just to desire instantaneous phenomenon encounters with heavenly beings. Seeing angels or other heavenly beings does not add value to your life after all. Rather, we should faithfully and continuously abide in our God-authored relationships with him, because he alone can change our lives forever. Even the Apostle Paul, who seemingly was very spiritual, only had one angelic appearance, and he did not even ask for it.

> For there stood by my side, last night, an angel of the God to whom I belong, and whom also I worship, and he said, "Dismiss all fear, Paul, for you must stand before Caesar; and God has granted you the lives of all who are sailing with you."
>
> Acts 27:23–24 (Weymouth)

God in his prerogative saw the fear and need in Paul's life and then decided to send him that angel to bring him assurance over the things he was worrying about.

Angels do not come to people to be watched, but to bring some specific messages. It is the message they bring that is more important than just seeing them. With this in mind, even those who go around claiming to have seen angels here and there need to scrutinize if what they see or have seen are genuine holy angels or just the many so-called angels common today, appearing even in people's closets and so forth.

31. *What can you say about angels of nations?*

Answer: Though there are popular notions and teachings about angels of nations, proper Scriptural studies only say this about Israel as a nation which had such a privilege when coming out of Egypt going to the Promised Land. In fact, the Hebrews thought that each nation had its guardian angel, with Michael who acts as the counsel for Israel's defense being her guardian angel. But the Bible does not directly say other nations have their angelic representatives! The book of Exodus talks so much about God sending his angel and angels to guide and guard, lead and fight, for the Israelites. Especially, the archangel Michael was greatly associated with Israel as a nation in the Old Testament. Some people think that is the reason Daniel was told, "and there is none that holdeth with me in these things, but Michael your prince" (Daniel 10:21). This seemed to indicate that Michael was the prince of the Hebrews in terms of angelic presence.

The Hebrews were a nation, but in the right sense of that word as used in the Bible, a people group and not a country or state. But much of what people imply today about angels of nations tends to mean angels of countries (states), being their own logical deductions. But the word *nation* as the Bible employs it comes from the word *ethnos*.

Thayer's Greek definitions say it is:

1. A multitude (whether of men or of beasts) associated or living together

   - a company, troop, swarm

2. A multitude of individuals of the same nature or genus

   - the human family

3. *A tribe, nation, people group*

4. In the Old Testament, foreign nations not worshipping the true God, pagans, Gentiles.

Strong's Hebrew and Greek Dictionary shows that it comes from the same root word *eth'-nos* and is defined as a race (as of the same habit), that is, a tribe; specifically a foreign (non-Jewish) one (usually by implication pagan); Gentile, heathen, nation, people.

From the above definitions and clarification, it is easy to presume that the groups that use the term *angels of nations* tend to mean nations as countries and not as people groups. But then the question arises as to what those angels' role (work) in those nations (countries) in relation to God's eternal purpose is. Did you know that a nation as a country may have many people groups (nations) in it? Considering the fact that nations (countries) are humans' own creations, what happens when a nation-state breaks up as happened in Russia? Does God add more angels to the resultant nations? Does Chechnya now have its new angel?

However, following the analysis of the Territorial and Strategic Spiritual Warfare Network groups, people come to some of these conclusions, especially concerning demonic spirits. But even if there are demon spirits over the world's cities, and countries; God is not in any competition with them warranting his deploying angels in those same cities to counter them! Sometimes people have this strange idea that God is in competition with Satan and his minions. But that is totally false; a god who competes with his creation or struggles to keep up with Satan cannot be the Almighty. Our God is working out his eternal divine purpose according to his own will not dependent on what Satan may be doing. He is up changing human beings one person at a time but working from within them; for the rich soil upon which the gospel takes root and grows is not the nation-states, but the individual human hearts. Someone has wisely stated that unless humans can be changed inwardly, external changes (even positioning angels in the air) will not make much difference in them.

Furthermore, the angels' objective in God's service toward man is to minister to individual people. Their mandate and term of reference is "to minister for them who shall be heirs of salvation" (Hebrews 1:14). There are no "nations" that are heirs of salvation, only individual persons within those nations! If angels are ministering spirits to minister to them who shall be heirs of salvation, how then can they minister to a nation or state wholesale? Doing that would contravene their very terms of reference and mandate that as we have seen, is to minister to individuals. And as a matter of known fact, angels do not function outside their specific given mandate. Yet, someone may object that I am trying to limit what God can do! However, I am not; God is God and can function as he pleases and whenever he deems fit within his eternal purposes, but in most cases he functions in agreement with his written word.

32. *You have so far spoken much on angels based on the premise that they are real. How about those who teach that there are no angels, claiming that they were just a creation of the early religious thinkers and Church fathers? Could they be right?*

Answer: I have spoken on angels as I have seen them in the Bible as real and true entities. However, sentiments and arguments to the effect that angels were just a creation of the early religious thinkers and Church fathers we have heard from many quarters. But such sentiments do not begin with the angel; it has everything to do with the writing of and the canonization of the Bible. Thus, *such sentiments are not an attack on the angels* per se *but an attack on the authority and reliability of the Bible as God's word.* What they claim of the angels as a creation of the religious minds and Church fathers of earlier centuries is the same claims they make of the Bible. Those who do not want to simply believe always claim that the Bible was the church fathers' creation and many such sentiments. Nonetheless, the Bible had to be written from somewhere somehow and so, were the various teachings that developed in the church then; God does not work in a cultural vacuum in relation to human life. It is such ancient cultural milieu what became important vehicles upon which the truth rode to eventually be transmitted to us as God's word, the Bible.

Furthermore, the Bible itself says that holy men were inspired by the Holy Spirit to write it. Men wrote, but it is God who gave them what to write and likewise with the angel teachings. It had to come from somewhere, be they cultural folklore or myths with backgrounds that were understandable then; otherwise you could not communicate effectively. Even Jesus while here on earth communicated in his preaching endeavors by referencing things like sheep, goats, mustard seeds, and so forth; the things people were familiar with.

But the major groups of those who claim that angels are not real are those influenced by the naturalistic worldview of science who claim that belief in things spiritual, like angels, is an outdated Gothic superstition that has no place in the modern times. They are biased towards rationalistic assumptions through which they reject the paradoxical evidence for spiritual reality. Yet theirs is a reaction to faith-based realities that cannot be easily corrected unless they come to faith since they are grounded on the naturalistic outlook to life that denies everything spiritual. They want everything scientifically proven or explained from the human standpoint before they can believe.

However, God and his spiritual realm including angels are very real, yet beyond scientific scrutiny; He can only be spiritually discerned according to the scriptures. For sure, he cannot be proven, investigated, or demonstrated by any human means, but must ultimately and confidently be accepted based on his own word (revelation) and paradoxical reality. Hence, people who aver that angels or spirits are not real are wrong. Theirs is just a claim they cannot prove either, as much as they would want us to prove angels. They also cannot prove that angels are not real. How can they prove that angels are not real, just by some arguments? Arguments cannot prove or disprove God or for that matter spiritual entities. There is need for more than just their rhetoric to be convinced that angels are not real. But they cannot offer that proof or any alternative and they are as wrong as people always are until illuminated by God's Spirit.

The Bible says the angel told Zacharias that he was Gabriel that stands before God.

> And the angel answering said unto him, I am Gabriel, that stand in the presence of God; and am sent to speak unto thee, and to show thee these glad tidings.
>
> Luke 1:19

Zacharias was a real person in Judea. God was real too, for he had heard Zacharias' prayers and dispatched an angel to bring him an answer. The angel God sent was also real, for he spoke to Zacharias, even introducing himself. This means the angel was conscious of who he was; he knew he existed. How could he not be real when he was conscious of his being? Furthermore, how can God send something that is just human imagination as is commonly claimed angels are? If they are not real entities, then the Bible is false for calling or referring to them as such. That even makes the angelic rescue of Peter in the book of Acts just a mere story. It means Peter was never arrested nor did the angel rescue him from the prison (Acts 12:1–11). It makes Paul's statement that God had sent him an angel in the ship on his way to Jerusalem a false claim (Acts 27:23–24). Even the angel that appeared to Gideon we can conclude was just a figment of his imagination; there was no real angel, and nothing even ate or received his sacrifice! Is that true? (Refer to Judges 6:11–22.)

If we adopt this paradigm and accept that angels are not real, then we have to go the whole length of finding new meanings to all the cases of angelic involvements or appearances in the Bible to have them make sense. Otherwise, we would be concurring with them that the Bible is not true.

Moreover, then how about people's personal encounters with angels that have been recounted the world over? Some of those encounters have totally had tremendous effects and changes on those who encountered these heavenly beings. Are those just other forms of make-believe? Take, for example, Zacharias' encounter with Gabriel that left him dumb for approximately nine months. Are we to brush that aside as a mere personal psychological experience that has no bearing on real life, yet it was a result of his angelic encounter? Only the unwarrantable skepticism and deeply prideful spirit (attitude) based on intellectual concerns can set such factors aside as exaggerations or myths. That is what the naturalists have always done, ignoring such examples as personal psychological occurrences that are not valid to all.

However, the intelligent thing to do in such cases is to thoroughly think such phenomena through as to what they tell us about ourselves, about God and his agents, because there is a connection. Yet denying such a connection does not obliterate it; it just leaves us in our ignorance of such matters. Thus, who should we believe; God expressing himself in his Word (the Bible) or the so-called learned men who are without God but always raise their opinions to contradict him? Do we want to believe in man or in God? Why would we put our faith in the weakness of human understanding that always changes?

Besides, even in some Christian circles, there are those who have been taught and conditioned that angels were just mere symbolical figures depicting various realities but were not realities themselves. Thus, with such a background and theological entrenchment, it is sad that such Christians also do not take the Bible literally when it comes to angels. But as they walk with God, he will bring them the right understanding and knowledge on this. We are not going to condemn or condone their position but trust that God who began the good work in them will bring them the necessary understanding.

Nonetheless, angels are real and about their business; people denying them or refusing to believe in them do not alter anything about them. I urge you to believe God's trustworthy and eternal Word and let those who want to doubt do so.

Epilogue

A word of caution will do some good; there is much angel talk and such related stuff going on these days. These increases in angelic or rather the supernatural involvements, most of it not the genuine godly manifestations, have burst forth due to increase in occult activities and the revival of the Eastern religions. These have opened floodgates of various teachings; some are clothed in Christian terminologies yet are still Eastern religious teachings at their core.

But any teaching though purported to be Christian that shifts your focus from God to some kind of an angel labeled "your angel" or something, may be dangerous to your faith in the long run. If the teaching makes you converse more with the *creature* than the *creator*, then you should begin to smell a rat. Any teaching that paints a picture of angels far above what the Bible clearly teaches about them should be shunned by all who truly love God.

For example, there are references in some literature that angels are responsible in helping people with their various needs, even with getting saved, or that angels bring people to a place they can make decision for Christ. However, gospel preaching to bring others to a place of decision for Christ is the work of human beings and not angels. By the workings of God, angels may orchestrate things to have you in a place to hear the gospel as happened to Cornelius (Acts 10), but they do not bring you into the place of decision for Christ. The gospel alone does that by the working of the Holy Ghost in your heart, not angels.

However, some Christian leaders themselves, especially the Strategic Warfare Network and some Prophetic groups, are the guiltiest in propagating wrong notions about angels. In the name of giving prophetic words, some leaders utter many unscriptural words that cannot be substantiated from the Bible. For example, I attended a conference where a charismatic so-called prophet prophesied to me saying, "God has opened a financial breakthrough for you, and he is sending angels to guard your finances; I can see them descending right now. Just believe this and nothing will happen to your finances. God has specifically put angels to guard them." I did not know what to think of that then, but basically I let the *prophet* talk; however, inwardly it did not register with my spirit.

In the same manner, a number of Christian leaders advise their followers or others to give or pray and God will send angels to meet their needs or lead them. However, such statements are not wholly true. As already observed, God mostly meets our needs through other people; it has always pleased him to use humans. He answers our prayers through fellow humans in most cases except in special situations.

Whereas in terms of God's leading a believer, he does not use angels; the story of Philip the evangelist, mightily used of God in Samaria, stands as an example. First God sent an angel to call him away from the revival he was involved with in that city. However, after that you never hear of that angel anymore. Philip was not led or guided by "his angel" but by God's Spirit (Acts 8:29). Angels can minister to us as God commands them, but in leading his people, God uses his Spirit (Romans 8:14).

Therefore, in this New Covenant Christianity there is no intermediary between God and man except the man Jesus Christ. Thus, if a teaching makes you pass through your angel, some saint, or the so-called "Virgin Mary" or any other route to God, then it is inconsistent with the New Covenant Christianity that Jesus constituted. That kind of teaching is false to true Christianity. Furthermore, God has no respect of persons; He will not hear Mary or anyone more than he will hear you. Why converse with an angel or anyone else when Christ (your advocate) is there ready for you, sitting at the right hand of the Father? He even promised to make his abode in you. Why ask your purported angel things concerning your life or future when he who holds the future is your Father? Why not just speak to God directly?

Some people have thrown caution to the wind in such matters and only discovered much later that they were trapped in things they voluntary got into. The beginnings of such involvements are often quite wonderful; some people even claim they are rewarding experiences, but alas the end thereof is the way of death. The Bible says:

> All the ways of a man are clean in his own eyes…and There is a way which seemeth right unto a man, but the end thereof are the ways of death.
>
> Proverbs 16:2a, 14:12

Hence, dear friend I trust you have enjoyed reading this book and I believe you have at least learned something new. But may I remind you to be cautious and sensible in all your ways and do not just accept everything because some good person has said them. Even the things I have shared in this book confirm from the Bible; do not just take my word for them. Study your Bible, pray for God's guidance and revelation, and prove all things. Enjoy grace and peace from God Almighty. Amen.

Contact
P.O. Box 18771
Seattle, WA 98118
or
ndugusijambo@gmail.com

listen|imagine|view|experience

AUDIO BOOK DOWNLOAD INCLUDED WITH THIS BOOK!

In your hands you hold a complete digital entertainment package. Besides purchasing the paper version of this book, this book includes a free download of the audio version of this book. Simply use the code listed below when visiting our website. Once downloaded to your computer, you can listen to the book through your computer's speakers, burn it to an audio CD or save the file to your portable music device (such as Apple's popular iPod) and listen on the go!

How to get your free audio book digital download:

1. Visit www.tatepublishing.com and click on the e|LIVE logo on the home page.
2. Enter the following coupon code:
   c47c-6bf2-1690-c2a2-2581-a993-cfc1-fd8b
3. Download the audio book from your e|LIVE digital locker and begin enjoying your new digital entertainment package today!